FREE 30-DAY M
CONTACTANYC

CELEBRITY LEVERAGE

Insider Secrets to Getting
Celebrity Endorsements,
Instant Credibility and
Star-Powered Publicity

Jordan McAuley
Foreword by Dan Kennedy

Mega Niche Media LLC
Los Angeles | New York

Celebrity Leverage: Insider Secrets to Getting Free Celebrity Endorsements, Instant Credibility, and Star-Powered Publicity

Copyright (c) 2010 by Jordan McAuley

Mega Niche Media LLC
8721 Santa Monica Blvd. #431
Los Angeles, CA 90069-4507
310-388-6084 (Phone & Fax)

www.MegaNiche.com

First Edition, 2010

Full Disclosure: This book contains affiliate links. Therefore, the author receives compensation for purchases made via these links.

ISBN: 978-1-60487-006-0

Printed in the United States of America

Design by Advantage Media Group

Cover by George Stevens

Praise for *Celebrity Leverage*

"Your credibility is the key to your success; this incredible book shows you how to 'hitch your wagon to a star' in your upward climb."

Brian Tracy, President
Brian Tracy International
Author of *The Way to Wealth* plus more than 45 business books

"*Celebrity Leverage* is your easiest, smartest, most cost-effective way to explode sales and set new records!"

Joe Vitale
Author of *The Attractor Factor* & contributor to *The Secret*

"You have in your hands a very valuable resource. It could lead to doubling or multiplying your income by a number of different means when you 'celebrity-ize' your business. Jordan is a very important voice to listen to on this subject."

Dan S. Kennedy
Glazer-Kennedy Inner Circle, Inc.
Author, *No B.S. Guide to Marketing to the Affluent*
plus many other business books

"Our society has become incredibly celebrity-centric and the media is giving more and more coverage to anything celebrity related. Jordan has put together a terrific book"

Yanik Silver, Founder
Maverick Business Adventures

"I was blown away at the many valuable tips in *Celebrity Leverage* that will dramatically enhance any marketing program, give you instant credibility, and drive sales. I strongly recommend this book—it should be a college course."

Joe Sugarman, Chairman
BluBlocker Corporation

"I tell my readers that the best way to improve marketing response rates is with endorsements. And the best way to use celebrity endorsements to improve your marketing results is by reading Jordan McAuley's excellent new book, *Celebrity Leverage*."

Bob Bly, Copywriter

"I've made millions of dollars leveraging and linking myself, my company, and my clients to famous people. Not only is it smart marketing—it's fun! Once you read this book, you'll have a step-by-step process for yourself. I call this ELF Marketing. That's easy, lucrative, and fun!"

Joe Polish, President
Piranha Marketing, Inc.

"This book ROCKS! I've long been aware of the power of marketing with celebrities, but had no idea how many easy ways there are to not only contact them, but use them to make yourself a lot more money! I'm going to buy copies for all my clients."

Ali Brown, CEO
Ali International, LLC

"With celebrity news and gossip hotter than ever, many authors, speakers, consultants, experts—even businesses and nonprofits—are leaving money on the table if they aren't trying their product, service, cause, or issue to celebrities. *Celebrity Leverage* shows you how with clever, creative ideas as well as helpful tips for getting past the gatekeepers."

Joan Stewart
The Publicity Hound

"Jordan's unique insight and information can do for your business what it has done for countless autograph enthusiasts' collections—namely, increasing its value, worth, and 'fun factor.' A must-have for anyone serious about competing in today's celebrity-driven markets."

Anthony D. Record, Contributing Editor
Autograph Magazine

"No matter what business you're in, you need celebrity endorsements, and Jordan McAuley is The Master at getting them! Double your business, double your credibility, and double your fun with this fabulous book!"

Sandy Grason
Sandy Grason Unlimited

"As an agency specializing in word-of-mouth marketing, we're always looking for ways to get the media and consumers talking. Prior to reading Jordan's book, we viewed celebrity association as a hit or miss prospect at best. This book has encouraged us to make use of celebrities in our clients' marketing plans to cut through the noise of conventional marketing."

Bill Balderaz, eMarketing Manager
ECNext.com

"Get the rich and famous to help make you rich and famous!"

Jess Todtfeld, President
Media Training Worldwide
Author of *Free Publicity*

"Jordan McAuley knows exactly how to reach the seemingly unreachable and now, with this book, he has outlined a simple and clear plan for you to do the same. *Celebrity Leverage* is the definitive guide to harnessing the power of celebrities to build incredible buzz about your product and service."

Donna Cutting, President
Donna Cutting Presents
Author of *The Celebrity Experience*

"This book is a must for any business that wants to leap ahead with the power of celebrity association. Jordan makes it easy for you to get started by teaching you how to get past the gatekeepers."

Chris Mullins, President
Phone Sales Doctor

"Want to utilize the appeal of celebrities to make your business or products stand out? You don't need to spend millions of dollars like Nike or Pepsi. Just read Jordan McAuley's *Celebrity Leverage*. You'll find out secrets any small business owner can use to benefit from 'celebrity power' for as little as the cost of postage. Buy this book now and follow Jordan's easy-to-implement advice. Then sit back and watch your sales skyrocket."

Mahesh Grossman, President
The Authors Team

"Hitching your marketing message to celebrities will skyrocket your power to influence many times over. Jordan McAuley shows you exactly how to use big-name star power in your business. Celebrity endorsements are easier than you think."

Susan Berkley, President
The Great Voice Company
Author of *Speak to Influence*

"Jordan McAuley is dedicated to providing in-depth details about the priceless opportunities celebrity association creates. He offers a wealth of information, including a comprehensive database of celebrity contacts, celebrity gift bag opportunities, success stories, expert interviews, and step-by-step guides on how to use these resources to grow your business."

Rebecca Lightsey, President
A Gifted Presence

"*Celebrity Leverage* is an invaluable tool for locating and securing celebrity endorsements to help market your product or service. When I obtained over 50 prestigious endorsements for my first book, the instant credibility quickly lead to key media including CNN, a PBS documentary, *Woman's Day*, *Prevention*, and an *AARP Bulletin* cover story. I'm now a sought-after international speaker, delivering 150 keynotes— including one to the Florida House of Representatives. Believe me—celebrity endorsements are priceless!"

Jacqueline Marcell
Author of *Elder Rage*

"Do you want more influence? Connections? Media coverage? Jordan McAuley has made it easy for you to get all of that, and a whole lot more, when you use the ideas, tools, and resources in his new book *Celebrity Leverage*. I invite you to get it right now, so you too can discover how to connect with, obtain, and use celebrity power."

Angela Treat Lyon
Author of *Keep on Track*

"This book is a valuable one. Jordan certainly has the credentials."

Michael Levine, President
Levine Communications
Author of *Guerilla PR Wired*

"Using celebrities and celebrity tie-ins are a couple of the absolute best ways to get free publicity, especially on the radio. This book tells you exactly how to capitalize on celebrities. It's an indispensable tool—I highly recommend it."

Alex Carroll
Author of *The Radio Publicity Manual*

"It's obvious. We lived in a celebrity-obsessed society. That can be turned into a HUGE jackpot for you. But, if you don't understand how it can benefit you, or how to use it to your advantage, you'll quickly be left in the dust. *Celebrity Leverage* will give you the jump, the lead, the advantage you need—and MUST have—in order to survive."

Paul Hartunian
Author of *101 Sizzling Hot Ways to Get Free Publicity*

"Celebrities = Attention. Trying to separate yourself and your business from the clutter is the hardest part of marketing. With celebrities, that hard work is done for you. My use of celebrities has made everything I do a lot easier. *Celebrity Leverage* is the authoritative guide for experts and a great introduction to those new to using celebrities."

Robert Skrob, President
Information Marketing Association
Co-Author of *The Official Get Rich Guide to Information Marketing*

"*Celebrity Leverage* is jam-packed with so many practical, interesting, and valuable up-to-the-minute ideas, insider tips, and important industry contacts to help one gain coveted media space and be a shining star in PR. I completely enjoyed reading it and highly recommend it."

Rhonda Rees, Former President
Los Angeles Publicity Club
Author of *Profit & Prosper with Public Relations*

Recommended Resources

BOOKS

The Celebrity Black Book:
More than 55,000 Accurate Celebrity Addresses
www.CelebrityBlackBook.com

Secrets to Contacting Celebrities:
101 Ways to Reach the Rich and Famous
www.SecretsToContactingCelebrities.com

DATABASES

Contact Any Celebrity
Membership Web site containing the complete contact information (best mailing address, agent, manager, publicist, and production company) for more than 59,000 celebrities and public figures worldwide.

www.ContactAnyCelebrity.com

The Celebrity Causes Database
Find out which celebrities contribute time and/or money to your charitable cause with this easy-to-use online database.

www.CelebCauses.com

TOOLKITS

Celebrity Book Endorsements Toolkit
www.BookEndorsements.com

Celebrity Endorsement Toolkit
www.CelebrityEndorsements.com

Acknowledgments

Along with family, friends, and associates, I'd like to thank the following for their generous support and faithful encouragement (in alphabetical order by last name):

Bill Balderaz, Susan Berkley, Alexandria Brown, Alex Carroll, Pauline Clifford, Jeff Crilley, Donna Cutting, Mike Esterman, Timothy Ferriss, Brian Patrick Flynn, Rick Frishman, Drew Gerber, Bill Glazer, Sandy Grason, Mahesh Grossman, Debra Englander, and the Authors Team for their help in organizing this work, Jake Halpern, Bill Harrison, Steve Harrison, Susan Harrow, Paul Hartunian, Robb Hecht, Craig Hirschfeld, Debra Holtzman, Dan Janal, Gavin Keilly, Dan Kennedy, John Kremer, Rebecca Lightsey, Beverly Mahone, Jacqueline Marcell, An Mathis Springs, Ann McIndoo, Lee Milteer, Gail Parenteau, Amy Peters, Joe Polish, Phyllis Pometta, Robin Quinn, Anthony D. Record, Rhonda Rees, Dr. Vail Reese, Brian Reich, Nick Romer, Corey Rudl, Robert Skrob, Tracy Sanders, Penny Sansevieri, Yanik Silver, Patrick Snow, Robyn Spizman, George Stevens, Joan Stewart, Amy Stumpf, Joe Sugarman, Jess Todtfeld, Brian Tracy, Angela Treat Lyon, Tsufit, Joe Vitale, Christine Williams, Adam Witty, and Anthony Zelig.

Disclaimer

This book is designed to provide information about marketing and publicity. It is sold with the understanding that the publisher and author are not engaged in rendering legal, accounting, financial or other professional services. If legal or other expert assistance is required, the services of a competent professional should be sought.

It is not the purpose of this book to reprint all the information that is otherwise available about marketing and publicity, but instead to complement, amplify, and supplement other texts. You are urged to read all the available material as much as possible and tailor the information to your individual needs.

Every effort has been made to make this manuscript as complete and accurate as possible. However, there may be mistakes, both typographical and in content. Therefore, this text should be used only as a general guide and not as the ultimate source of information. Furthermore, this manuscript contains information that's current only up to the printing date.

The purpose of this book is to educate and entertain. The author and publisher shall have neither liability nor responsibility to any person or entity with respect to loss or damage caused, or alleged to have been caused, directly or indirectly, by the information contained in this book.

CELEBRITY LEVERAGE

Insider Secrets to Getting Celebrity Endorsements, Instant Credibility and Star-Powered Publicity

Jordan McAuley

Foreword by Dan Kennedy

Table of Contents

PART II:
Making *Yourself* Famous..................... 123

Introduction

What *Celebrity Leverage* Can Do for You...

Throughout these pages, you'll discover creative strategies for getting your products in celebrities' hands, getting low-cost and free celebrity endorsements, linking your business, product or service to celebrities in other ways, and even making yourself into a celebrity. All of these strategies are what I collectively call "Celebrity Leverage."

This book is divided into two parts. The first, "Making Your Business Famous," shows you how to get other celebrities to promote your business, your products, and your services.

In Part I, you'll learn how to:

- Get your products in celebrities' hands
- Get your products in celebrity gift bags, suites and lounges
- Get free and low-cost product placement (on TV and film)
- Contact celebrities (by mail, in person, and online)
- Hold a celebrity-themed event
- Hire celebrities for events (as hosts, performers and speakers)

The second section of *Celebrity Leverage*, "Making Yourself Famous," reveals how to turn yourself into a celebrity in your area, your niche and your field.

In Part II, you'll discover how to:

Become a celebrity expert in the media

- Get on television (reality TV, QVC, and yes...even *Oprah*.)

- Appear in magazines, newspapers, and on radio

- Write a best-selling book

- Maximize press coverage

- Generate buzz using Web 2.0 (blogs and social networking)

Along with insider secrets from myself, you'll also hear advice from some of today's top marketing and publicity experts.

Remember that all the topics above are possible for your business, and successfully implementing just one is enough to skyrocket your sales and multiply your income. Try not to get overwhelmed by all the possibilities as you explore *Celebrity Leverage*. You don't have to do everything at once. The key is to simply take action and *get started*.

I look forward to hearing about all of your Celebrity Leverage success stories. Please drop me a line at jordan@contactanycelebrity.com.

Reach for the stars,

Jordan McAuley
Founder & President
Contact Any Celebrity &
CELEBRITY | PR

P.S.—Be sure to claim your free 30-day membership to Contact Any Celebrity for instant access to constantly-updated contact information for more than 59,000 celebrities and public figures worldwide.

www.contactanycelebrity.com/free

Foreword

"I'm saddened by how few marketers utilize opportunities
for free celebrity marketing; linking to currently popular
TV programs, movies, and celebrities."

Dan Kennedy
No B.S. Marketing to the Affluent

DanKennedyPresents.com

I tell my readers, subscribers, and clients that "celebrity association" is NOT an option. Today, celebrities dominate the news, the water cooler conversation, and everyone's mind space, whether CEO of a Fortune 500 corporation or suburbia soccer mom. It used to be that celebrity news was relegated to the tabloids and a few entertainment shows on television. Today, celebrities grace the covers of *Fortune* just as they do the *National Enquirer*, and their activities lead the news on CNN.

At my urging, countless clients—national companies marketing directly to consumers or business to business—have in one way or another associated themselves with celebrities and profited from doing so. At first, many thought this was beyond their reach. Maybe you do, too. Well, *it isn't*.

Companies selling to the most affluent consumers, offering such goods as luxury cars, fractional jet ownership, and multimillion-dollar condos or other investments, as well as companies selling to "ordinary Joes and Janes" such things as weight-loss programs, fashion, cosmetics, even prescription drugs from "the little blue pill" to "the little purple pill," scurry to sign up celebrities for their advertising...*because it works.*

Jordan McAuley is an astute, experienced and highly respected expert in both the sourcing and effective use of celebrities for business promotion. His is an important voice on this subject, and you have in your hands a valuable resource. It could lead to doubling or multiplying your income by a number of means. Consider this:

- Celebrity association can make it possible to charge premium prices and fees and sell at prices significantly higher than your competitors or the industry norms—with no other changes in your goods, services, advertising, marketing or sales. That obviously increases income.

- You can get more and better word-of-mouth advertising or "buzz" and more referrals. Celebrity association reduces your need to buy advertising and lowers your overall costs of acquiring customers. There's abundant evidence that adding celebrities to advertising boosts readership, listenership and viewership, thus making each dollar invested produce more.

- Pricey, exclusive night clubs, restaurants and resorts pay large "appearance fees" to have celebrities come so they can brag about it. This can filter down to local businesses as well. Among my clients, a local spa brought in two soap opera stars for its grand opening; a local restaurant made itself the talk of the town with a "guest TV celebrity chef" event; and a local mortgage broker in Chicago helped his income soar by using the immensely popular William "Refrigerator" Perry, the retired Chicago Bears player, in all his direct mail and even in voice messages delivered to customers.

- My long-time client, the Guthy-Renker corporation, was the first to bring celebrity hosts to TV infomercials and has continually upped that ante, building its franchise brands in skin care with Jessica Simpson, Vanessa Williams, Victoria Principal, Sean "Diddy" Combs, and soap opera stars. The largest public seminar company with which I toured as a speaker (for nine years) brought more than a hundred celebrities to its stage, so I appeared repeatedly with not only four former U.S. presidents and Generals Colin Powell and Norman Schwarzkopf, but also Bill Cosby, Mary Tyler Moore, Naomi Judd, Johnny Cash and Christopher Reeve.

- I have decades of experience using celebrities in advertising, marketing, promotion, personal appearances, and in other ways for myself and for my clients. It has, almost without exception, been positive and profitable. The list is far too long for this Foreword, but on it are celebrities such as Donald and Ivanka Trump; George Ross; Kristi Frank and Bill Rancic from *The Apprentice*; Gene Simmons of KISS; George Foreman, Mike Ditka and Jim Palmer from the world of sports; hundreds of best-selling authors; and many stars from film and television.

Celebrities are available to fit just about any reasonable budget and for just about any purpose, and Jordan McAuley is one of the few guys on the planet who really knows how to get them. His advice and sources are invaluable. Beyond outright "renting" celebrities, there are many other ways to link yourself, your products, your services and your business to them: charities, speaking on the same venue, even by being alert for news articles in which celebrities talk about your type of business.

If you're attentive, you'll recognize the dominating command that "celebrity" has on every strata of society, every media in our culture, and every conversation. If you're astute, you'll recognize the importance of not having your businesses unattached and left out of this powerful and pervasive influence on the conversations of the day and buying decisions of virtually every consumer of everything.

The movement of celebrities and celebrity news from the sideshow of entertainment to the main stage of politics, business and finance is a mandate. If you're not actively and creatively linking your business to celebrities, you're ignoring the single most significant trend in advertising and marketing of our times.

Dan S. Kennedy is the author of the popular "No B.S." series with such titles as *No B.S. Marketing to the Affluent*, *No B.S. Wealth Attraction for Entrepreneurs*, *No B.S. Business Success*, and *No B.S. Direct Marketing for Non-Direct Marketing Businesses*. He is also a highly successful serial entrepreneur who has built, bought and sold a number of businesses. Through a network of consultants, his own consulting and coaching programs, and his four different business newsletters, Dan Kennedy influences more than one million business owners each year.

Free Bonus Gift!

A unique Free Bonus Gift including two months of Dan Kennedy's most popular marketing newsletter plus $613.91 of pure, powerful, money-making, business-life-altering information is available to readers of this book at www.DanKennedyPresents.com.

PART I:

Making Your Business Famous

"Every day, Hollywood celebrities work hard to create some new opportunity for you, some new attention-grabbing "hook" you can use. Every dumb thing they say, every outrageous thing they do, every news event they're a part of may provide you with an advertising or publicity angle. How often do you capitalize on these things?"

Dan Kennedy
No B.S. Marketing to the Affluent

www.DanKennedyPresents.com

In the introduction to his book *The Long Tail*, Chris Anderson underscores our obsession with celebrity when he says:

"We define our age by our celebrities and mass-market products—they are the connective tissue of our common experience now spun out of every corner of commerce, from shoes to chefs. Our media is obsessed with what's hot and what's not."

Such burgeoning curiosity regarding celebrities is about more than their performance and daily movements past the public eye. We also care about what they eat, what they wear, where they vacation, and more. And this interest isn't only a trend among adults. The highly coveted "tween" market cares as well. According to *Entrepreneur* magazine, 72 percent of children ages 10 to 13 ("tweens") say that seeing their favorite celebrity use a brand makes them want to use it as well.

Today it's more important than ever to associate your business, your product, and yourself with celebrities—and even make yourself into a celebrity—to rise above the competition. As Dan Kennedy says:

"Celebrities DOMINATE every aspect of media, every demographic. Surely, what works selling to the blue-haired little old ladies in the magazines they read while sitting under the hair dryers at the beauty parlor couldn't possibly influence executives with MBAs and cigar chompin', street-wise business owners running trucking companies. If you're honest and intelligent, you'll see that there's NO difference. Celebrity-izing your business is NOT an option."

There are multiple ways you can quickly and easily "celebrity-ize" your business. You don't have to do them in any particular order, and you don't have to do all of them. Each component acts as a snowball.

If you can just get a couple of them rolling, your results will grow by themselves. Consider the possibilities...

You get your product into the hands of a hot Hollywood celebrity, who wears or carries it on the red carpet or talks to the media about loving it. Or you get written up in a local magazine, which prompts other magazines and newspapers to cover you (media begets media). Or you write a book that hits the best-seller list, selling millions of copies while promoting you. Or a celebrity expert gives you an endorsement or testimonial. Or your product is featured on a hit TV show or in a blockbuster movie, and suddenly everyone wants it.

Success Story: Magnolia Bakery

One small business that's been extremely successful "celebrity-izing" itself is Magnolia Bakery (www.MagnoliaCupcakes.com) on Bleecker Street in New York City. The bakery is known for its Depression-era inspired icebox cakes, but it is most famous for its cupcakes.

Alyssa Torey and Jennifer Appel opened Magnolia Bakery in 1996. They are credited with starting a "cupcake craze" in the '90s that has recently resurfaced. How did they do this? By using five main "Celebrity Leverage" tactics.

First, they created a quality product. Without that, nothing else would matter.

Second, they created a "velvet rope." There's usually a line to get into Magnolia Bakery, and a "cupcake bouncer" actually guards the door to let in only a few people at a time. Cupcake purchases are limited to 12 per customer because of their popularity.

Third, they wrote a book. In 1999, the two published *The Magnolia Bakery Cookbook: Old-Fashioned Recipes from New York's Sweetest Bakery*. This opened the door for media coverage and positioned Alyssa and Jennifer as experts on cupcakes and the owners of one of New York City's best bakeries.

Fourth, they've gone after media coverage. Magnolia has been featured in almost all of New York's local media like *New York Magazine*, plus national media like *USA Today*, the Food Network, and more.

Fifth, they appeared on TV and in movies. In 2005, Magnolia Bakery and its cupcakes were featured in a *Saturday Night Live* digital short. But they secured their celebrity status with appearances on *Sex and the City* and *The Devil Wears Prada*. In fact, the bakery is now one of the 40 featured stops of On Location Tour's (www.ScreenTours.com) *Sex and the City* Hotspots. The tour now drops off buses of new customers every day at the famous bakery.

As Magnolia manager Margaret Hathaway told *USA Today* after the bakery appeared in *Sex and the City*, "Fans come in all the time asking for whatever it is that Sarah Jessica Parker was eating."

Celebrity Leverage Can Work for You, Too.

Big brands are cashing in, and you should, too. By following the many strategies I'll reveal in this book, you'll soon see that it's entirely possible to get your product or service promoted by celebrities in ways you never imagined.

To gain Celebrity Leverage, you don't have to spend millions of dollars to get Jessica Simpson to say she loves your product in an infomercial. You don't have to be Coca-Cola to get your product featured on TV shows and in movies. The truth is, there are many low-cost and even free ways to get your products into the hands of celebrities and endorsed by them, with or without their knowing.

Take, for instance, my clients such as the jewelry designer who was able to get her designs worn by the cast of a major TV show popular among teenagers, without paying for product placement. Or consider the shoe designer who got her creations into the hands of Paris Hilton—then spotted photos of the heiress wearing them on the red carpet. Or the teddy bear maker who received thank you notes from Sarah Jessica Parker, Brooke Shields and other stars. Or the baby products company that spotted Angelina Jolie, Brad Pitt, Gwen Stefani and others using their baby carriers in major celebrity magazines. Or the massage therapist who set up his table at a soap opera star's birthday party and gave massages to her and all her soap opera star friends.

You're probably thinking that all of these people—and trust me, there are many more just like them—must have had some sort of Hollywood connections. They must have had a family member or a friend in the business, right? Wrong. What they did was use some of the insider tips, tricks, and techniques that I reveal in this book. I'll show you exactly how they did it–and how you can, too.

Celebrity Leverage will show you many ways to tie your business, your product, and even yourself to celebrities. You'll also learn how to elevate your business, your product, and yourself to celebrity status. Although I'll share many tactics for these approaches that you can implement for free, I'll also reveal some of the paid opportunities that are available. Of course, "celebrity-izing" your business is pointless if you don't leverage your success, so I'll also cover how to effectively maximize the publicity you receive.

Who Am I, Anyway?

When I was younger, I enjoyed writing to celebrities and requesting auto-graphed photos. Stars would usually respond to my letters, so I began collecting autographs for fun (eventually getting several hundred). To help other collectors, I started building a Rolodex of celebrity contacts that worked. In 1996, I founded my business, Contact Any Celebrity (www.ContactAnyCelebrity.com), a service that provides celebrity contact information to fans, businesses, nonprofits, authors, and the media–while I was in film school at the University of Miami.

While I was in film school, I interned at CNN and Turner Entertainment during the summers and also at a prominent modeling agency in South Beach, Miami. In addition to what I was learning in my film classes, these jobs gave me a "real world" view into how entertainment companies and talent agencies really worked. As soon as I graduated, I moved to Los Angeles, where I immediately landed a job at a Hollywood film production company. After working there for a while, I was offered a job as an agent's assistant at a top Beverly Hills talent agency. That's where I learned from both my boss and the guys in the mailroom what gets past the gatekeepers and into the hands of celebrities–and how anyone can do it.

While working at the agency, however, my Contact Any Celebrity business continued to grow. Soon, I had to make a choice between the two jobs because I couldn't keep up with both. So I chose to grow Contact Any Celebrity. Today my online database contains the best USPS-verified mailing address, agent, manager, publicist, production company and charitable cause for more than 59,000 celebrities and public figures worldwide. Everyone who is anyone is included. But don't take my word for it–visit www.ContactAnyCelebrity.com now to search our rolodex and see for yourself.

More than 5,000 small businesses, brand-name companies, authors, publicists, journalists and marketers use Contact Any Celebrity daily, many for getting their products to celebrities. In addition to contact information, we also provide a constantly updated listing of celebrity gifting opportunities at award shows and events so businesses can easily get their products and services into the hands of celebrities.

Open the Velvet Rope!

OK, now I'm going to open the velvet rope and let you in the door to an exciting new world of marketing and publicity opportunities by using celebrities. Since the adventure we're about to embark on is about celebrity-izing you and your business, a bit of Hollywood fun will be added to the mix. Along the way, you'll hear not only from myself, but also from other top marketing and publicity experts.

CHAPTER 1

Creating A Celebrity Experience

"How far are you willing to go to say 'yes' to your customers?"

Donna Cutting
The Celebrity Experience

A recognized expert on personalized customer service, Donna Cutting (www.DonnaCutting.com) studies the unique ways that celebrities are treated as customers, compared with most people. She also studies companies that regularly service celebrities to learn what they do to attract the rich and famous. She writes about this in her new book, *The Celebrity Experience*.

Insider Interview: Donna Cutting, Donna Cutting Presents

JORDAN MCAULEY: What is the biggest difference between the service celebrities receive and the service the rest of us get?

DONNA CUTTING: Scott Graham, the CEO of Extreme Personal Assistant Concierge Services (www.GoXPACS.org), told me a great story that is the first chapter of the book. His "Chicago Pizza Story" about a new celebrity client lays the foundation for everything I talk about.

This new client was testing what Scott's Web site says: "If you can imagine it, we can deliver it." He promises right on his Web site that as long as it's moral, ethical, and legal, they'll do it for you.

The celebrity called Scott up and said, "Here's what I want: a hot, fresh pizza delivered at 5 p.m. to my home from a specific pizza parlor in Chicago to my flat in London." Now when most people hear this, they immediately think, "Impossible!"

What XPACS did, however, was put a pizza oven onto a private plane along with one of their concierges. They flew the private jet to London, cooking the pizza on the way down. The limo was waiting, and at 5 p.m., the celebrity had his pizza right on time in London direct from Chicago.

To me, this shows the difference between what celebrities get and the rest of us. Whatever the celebrity wants, the answer is "yes." The first objection I hear when I talk about this is, "Of course the answer is yes. This guy probably has billions of dollars and can afford to have a pizza put on a private plane." That is true, and most customers do not have that kind of money. However, what we can learn from this story is how many times in customer service we tell the customer "no" when there are other options.

For instance, I called a business the other day to ask for directions. I said, "Can you please tell me what the nearest cross-street is to your business?" And the customer service rep said, "I don't know." He could have asked someone else. He could have pulled GoogleMaps up on his computer. But that was the end of the conversation

The difference between the celebrity service companies and those who give substandard service is that the celebrity service companies say "yes" and then figure out how.

JM: W Hotels (www.WHotels.com) does this with their "Whatever, Whenever" service. Is this type of customer service a new trend?

DC: It's a trend with businesses who really get it. There are companies who promise this type of service and don't really deliver it. The difference is the attitude of, "Yes, we can do this, and this is who we're going to be. This is what we choose to be as a company and the kind of service we choose to provide."

The W is a great example. I talked to one of the concierges at the W and asked him, "What's the strangest thing you've ever been asked for?" He said he literally gave a guest the shirt off his back one day because the gentleman had gotten a stain and needed a new one. Right there at the concierge desk, the employee took his shirt off and gave it to the customer.

JM: Tell me about the plumber in your book.

DC: I found Hub Plumbing (www.HubPlumbing.com) because they literally say they give red carpet customer service. If you look them up, it says it on their Web site.

John Wood, the company's CEO, decided that he didn't want to be like every other plumber. When John started out, he noticed how nervous female customers looked when he arrived at their homes because they were letting a strange man in. So he began to think, "How can I be different? How can I change the perception of what plumbers are?" He developed this organization from the get-go. Now he's expanded with eight to ten technicians working for him along with people in the office

When you call Hub Plumbing, there's a live person available 24/7 who answers the phone. If you do this, you're already above all the other businesses who just send customers to voicemail. The employees who answer Hub Plumbing's phones are trained very well. They're answering questions for the caller before he or she even asks any.

After the appointment is set up for the technician to come to your house, you receive an e-mail from your plumber. It has a photograph of the specific technician who's going to come to your residence. It tells you information about him, not only professional but also personal, like how many kids he has. You already have a relationship with this person and you know what he looks like before he ever shows up.

When the Hub Plumbing technician arrives, he drives up in a beautiful, shiny red truck and calls to let you know he's there. After you invite him in, he literally rolls out a red carpet, plus puts shoe covers on. When he gets to the work area, he lines up his plumbing tools as if they were surgical instruments.

After the job is finished, you receive a handwritten thank you note from your plumber, thanking you for allowing them to do the job. They also follow up with a phone call to find out if you were satisfied with everything. Of course, 99 percent of the time people are not only satisfied but they're also blown away because they have never had this type of service experience with a plumber before.

JM: A big part of this is about making the customer feel special.

DC: You hit the nail on the head. Sometimes with customer service, what people end up doing is fixing problems in the name of customer service. They make a mistake, and when the customer complains, they come back and fix the problem right away. Then they say, "We give good customer service."

It's reactive as opposed to proactive. Giving the celebrity experience is how we proactively create a positive experience for our customers.

JM: How can someone quickly add celebrity service to his or her business?

DC: First, the foundation for this whole idea is having the attitude of "Yes we can."

Second, give them the chicken soup. We often hear about the riders that celebrities have in their contracts for specific demands backstage or on sets. They want only Evian water, for example. These are things that for whatever reason make the celebrity feel comfortable wherever he or she is.

I recently had a conversation with Jack Canfield (www.JackCanfield.com) who helped create the *Chicken Soup for the Soul* series. He certainly has some celebrity status. When he goes places, people do things for him that they wouldn't necessarily do for someone else.

For example, Jack went to a hotel once while he was on a book tour. In his room, the hotel had a canister of hot chicken soup sitting there for him with a bowl, a napkin, a spoon, and a little note that said, "Chicken soup for Jack Canfield's body and soul." He said the fact that they took the time to know who he was, to demonstrate that in a tangible way, really made a difference. It made him remember the people at the hotel.

Third, find creative ways to use your customers' names, and make that a major part of your customer service. High Point University is profiled in the book as one of the Celebrity Experience Hall of Fame members. One of the things they do is when prospective students come to visit the university, his or her parking space says, "High Point University Welcomes Jordan," for example. Students and their families actually stand by their car and take a picture. They've already visited five or six colleges, and none of them have done anything like that before. So what are you willing to do? How far are you willing to go to say "yes" to your customers?

Create a Velvet Rope

One way to create both demand and allure is to create a "velvet rope" around your business. If you've ever been to a popular nightclub where only those whose names are "on the list" or the bouncer chooses to let inside are granted access, you know how maddening it feels not to be allowed in.

When I was studying film business at the University of Miami, my friends and I drove to South Beach almost every weekend to try to get into the hottest clubs. Sometimes we were on the list because we knew the bouncer or promoter who was in one of our classes, and sometimes we were just trying to get in on our own.

I noticed a few interesting things about this kind of exclusive atmosphere where only the wealthiest, most beautiful, and most connected were welcomed.

One, it attracted a high level of clientele. Models fought over eachother, pushing themselves up front to get noticed. Investment bankers flaunted their wealth, and social climbers dropped every name in the book. If you weren't good-looking, rich or connected, what was the point? Some didn't even try to get in.

To learn more about how to create a velvet rope, check out Dan Kennedy's (www.DanKennedyPresents.com) luxury *Marketing: The No B.S. Marketing to the Affluent Newsletter* (dankennedy.com/luxury) and Ryan Lee's (RyanLee.com) *Velvet Rope Fitness Marketing* (VelvetRopeFitnessMarketing.com). Even if you're not in the fitness industry, you'll still learn many new techniques including the "Nine Secret Laws of the Velvet Rope" and how to make them work for you!

Second, it allowed the clubs to charge higher prices. Most of the people who got past the velvet rope had money to burn, or at least someone in their group had money. The difference between a $35 cover and a $5 cover and a $25 cocktail or a $5 cocktail didn't matter to them. What I also overheard many times was: "We went through this much trouble to get in, so we might as well pay."

Third, these were the clubs that attracted all the media attention—and all the celebrities. The media didn't cover and celebrities didn't frequent the non-exclusive clubs—only the ones with a real "velvet rope" factor.

Marc Benecke, the bouncer of Studio 54 during its heyday, witnessed people do all sorts of things to try to get past his velvet rope and into the infamous New York City nightclub it guarded. Thomas Onorato, author of *Confessions from the Velvet Rope*, told the *Palm Beach Post* that those things included "a man who died trying to sneak in through a vent, a woman who took off all her clothes, and a newlywed who got the nod but left his bride outside."

Your velvet rope doesn't have to be a physical one. For example, toy companies create a velvet rope every year right before Christmas. They promote the hottest new product like crazy, then conveniently run out of it right before Christmas Eve, causing parents to do whatever they can to get one—many times behaving not so Christmas-like! Of course this creates a ton of publicity—and a bunch of disappointed children on Christmas morning. But just a few days later, the toy is back in stock and when everyone is returning what they don't want to the stores, it sells out yet again.

There are three main ways to create a velvet rope:

1. Actually have a velvet rope. Nightclubs do this all the time. This approach might work for your business, too. Simply putting a velvet rope outside your entrance—at least for openings and special events—will make people walking by to want to know what's going on, automatically drawing a crowd.

2. Limit access. You can also create a velvet rope by limiting supply. An Mathis Springs, known as the "crab cake lady", makes customers come to her South Carolina store in person, refusing to ship or sell her homemade crab cakes on the Internet. Magnolia Bakery in New York City has a "cupcake bouncer" guarding the door, allowing onlya a certain number of customers in at a time.

3. Create a social network. You've heard of MySpace (www.MySpace.com) and Facebook (www.Facebook.com). But did you know that there are a myriad of specialized social networks? There's Dogster.com for dog lovers, Catster.com for cat lovers, and more. Something to think about: Seth Godin (www.SethGodin.com), author of the book *Tribes,* says: "Who you leave out is just as important as who you let in." Services like Ning (www.Ning.com) make creating social networks a breeze for your business.

CHAPTER 2:

Linking to Celebrities

"If you can associate your business with a
celebrity, you will make more money."

Bill Glazer, President
Glazer-Kennedy Insider's Circle
www.DanKennedyPresents.com

The number one question most business people ask me is, "How can I get my product or service to celebrities?" The good news is you can. The bad news is...well, there isn't any, really, *unless* you're not willing to put in the work (and sometimes some money as well.)

The Benefits of Linking to Celebrities

Who exactly is swayed by celebrities? Just about everyone.

Housewives are influenced by *Oprah's Favorite Things* episodes and celebrities pitching their products on QVC. Businessmen are swayed by Pamela Anderson and Jenny McCarthy appearances at trade shows. And teenagers are won over by Jessica Simpson, Vanessa Williams, and Diddy in ProActive commercials.

Don't underestimate the teen market, either. According to a recent *USA Today* article, "Generation Y, those between about 8 and 26, are considered the most important generation for retailers and marketers because of their spending power and the influence they have over what their parents buy."

Today's culture, from politics to fashion to music to sports, is celebrity-driven. Virtually every large corporation has some tie-in to a celebrity.

There are five main reasons why you need to "celebrity-ize" your business:

1. Using celebrities adds instant credibility. The customer, consciously or unconsciously, believes: "If a celebrity is using this product, it must be good because they can get whatever they want." You can then charge higher prices.

2. Using celebrities gets people to pay attention. That's why infomercials and commercials use celebrities all the time. They can make the viewer stop flipping channels if he or she notices a major celebrity in a commercial.

3. Using celebrities provides enhanced credibility. People trust celebrities they like and admire. They figure, "This celebrity has his or her choice of all the products in the world, so there must be a good reason for choosing this one." Most people also trust celebrities—especially those who appear on television—like their friends. After all, celebrities we enjoy watching on TV every day or every week come into our homes more than our friends probably do.

4. Using celebrities often leads to increased media exposure. The media knows people pay attention to celebrities, so they are more likely to feature your product or service.

5. It's fun. We all know running a business can have its good days and bad days, and sometimes it gets repetitive and it's just not that much fun. Using celebrities will most likely add a new level of fun for you, your employees, and your customers.

As a business person, you're well aware of how competitive your market is. You need to have an edge if your product or service is going to stand out from the crowd. Using celebrities helps achieve this. With the right celebrity, your product or service will be immediately viewed as exclusive and distinctive—something everyone wants to have.

Insider Interview: Jake Halpern, Author

Few people have looked as deeply at the impact and influence of celebrity on our culture than Jake Halpern (www.JakeHalpern.com), NPR commentator and the author of *Fame Junkies*. Jake studied why celebrities have such a powerful impact on people and culture.

JORDAN MCAULEY: Explain why the obsession with fame may be hard-wired into our brains.

JAKE HALPERN: The question I get asked so much is, "Why are we so crazy about celebrities?" People want magic bullet answers, but I don't think there are any. I think it's a combination of forces, and one of these forces is evolution. While researching *Fame Junkies*, I went down to Duke University and met with Dr. Michael Platt, a neurobiologist who studies Rhesus monkeys.

He explained that in any troop of monkeys and generally in a lot of primates, there is a dominant monkey—the classic alpha male—and that monkey demands tribute from the other monkeys. The other monkeys bow down and grab onto him. It's all very celebrity-like.

In one experiment, Dr. Platt built a device that gauged where the monkeys looked. They had two options: one was they could get food and the other was they could stare at a picture of the dominant monkey in their group. What he found was, again and again, the monkeys actually gave up food in order to stare at the dominant monkey—and they paid a price for it.

Dr. Platt explained that our brains are hard-wired to zone in on the powerful, important players in our circle. Back in ancient cave times, we studied the dominant person in our cave and when they ate, what they ate, where they slept, who they slept with, and what they did at different times of the day. And we were careful observers of this.

This behavior increased the chance that we would survive and therefore pass along the genes that make us watch important people. Then, over time, the gene created a mechanism that told our brains, "Hey, watch that guy strutting around or watch that sexy woman." So now we can kind of understand why our minds are hijacked by pop culture.

Instead of watching the movers and shakers of our immediate circle, we're watching celebrities because they're strutting self-important, flamboyant behavior. It triggers the part of our brain that says, "Hey, watch that person, because he or she is important for your own survival." But as we know, watching Tom Cruise jump up and down on Oprah's couch isn't exactly important for our survival. But that ancient mechanism is still firing away in our brains.

JM: Celebrity news circulations are skyrocketing, but real news magazines aren't doing so well.

JH: That's absolutely right. Magazines like *Entertainment Weekly*, *Us Weekly*, and *Star* have grown. Their circulations are absolutely through the roof. But magazines like *Time* and *Newsweek* are totally stagnant. This is part of an even larger trend as well. The conventional, mainstream media follows celebrity stories now in a way they didn't do ten years ago. Outlets like CNN, the *New York Times*, and the Associated Press, that normally have avoided celebrity news as being too frivolous or fluffy, have now jumped into it over their heads.

JM: Why do you think celebrities help products sell?

JH: The best-selling grill and one of the most profitable celebrity endorsements of all time is the George Foreman Grill, which is kind of bizarre. What does George Foreman know about electric grills?

It's a number of things. One is we feel we know these celebrities. We have faith in the names of these people. We are invested in them. Whether we know it or not, there's a sense of trust and a sense of similarity. We "know" George Foreman; he seems like a nice guy. We remember him in the Dunkin' Donuts commercials where he was trying to get back in shape to fight the title. He was always dealing with weight himself. He was a good 'ol guy out in your backyard cooking. We don't know any of this for sure, but we feel it, and those feelings seep into the products.

On the one hand, there's a sense of trust: We feel that celebrities would not be endorsing some crack-pot product because they have to protect their own name. So it has to be somewhat decent. We also want the illusion of being close to them because we can say, "I have the same purse as she dos" or "I have the same sneakers as him." To some extent, it's an illusion of proximity. We feel we're as good as they are, or at least close to what they are, because we have their stuff.

The other point to realize is that this isn't always conscious. It's often all working subconsciously as we're making the decision. I'm not actively thinking, "This is why I'm buying the George Foreman Grill." It's more of just the feeling we have, but the feelings have these specific reasons, and it's interesting that we have these feelings for people we don't really even know.

Dan Kennedy (www.DanKennedyPresents.com), author of *Marketing to the Affluent*, knows from considerable experience how much of an impact using celebrities in marketing can have:

"America is *obsessed* with celebrities. The serious news publications are floundering while the celebrity gossip publications are growing at a pace as high as 100 percent a year. Looking at this in isolation from context, you might make the arguments of gender, supermarket newsstand vs. bookstore and airport newsstands, etc. But in context, there's no argument left. An increasing percentage of time on CNN, MSNBC, FNN, even on the financial news programs, is about celebrities. Business magazines do celebrity covers. Look around. It's everywhere.

"Celebrities DOMINATE every aspect of media, every demographic. Surely, what works selling to the blue-haired little old ladies in the magazines they read while sitting under the hair dryers at the beauty parlor couldn't possibly influence executives with MBAs and cigar chompin', street-wise business owners running trucking companies. If you're honest and intelligent, you'll see that there's NO difference."

Before you start attaching your products and services to celebrities, make sure you choose the proper ones for your business. This is vitally important. Often, these may be celebrities you're not aware of or even stars you're not a big fan of. I'll explain why the right choice is so important, along with how to choose the best celebrities to make your business famous, in the next chapter.

CHAPTER 3

Choosing the Right Celebrities

"Social proof is a very powerful subliminal persuader. This is increasingly true the higher the stature of the person delivering the testimonial."

Dave Lakhani
Author of Subliminal Persuasion

It may take some time and effort to find the right celebrity (or combination of celebrities) for your venture. However, this is an extremely important step. Even if you're fortunate enough to have a celebrity friend or family member, you should spend some time thinking about the relationship the celebrity will have with your product and your customers.

A celebrity attachment is a bit like a marriage—or really a marriage with extended family—because your customers are involved also. And like all personal and professional relationships, you need to be ready for the possible ups and downs of this business arrangement along with any disagreements that could arise down the road.

So, how do you pick the best celebrity to tie into your business? If you're just starting out, you may not have the budget to hire a big star for a television campaign. But as you'll learn throughout this book, there are ways to tie a celebrity to your product without having to hire one.

Keep in mind that it doesn't have to be a huge Hollywood star. If you run a car dealership, you could connect with a local sports legend or radio host in your town. Consider what type of public figure will best help sell your product, who will be genuinely interested in it, and who is likely to influence your customers because they already have an emotional connection to that celebrity.

Here are some tools to help you out.

Tools for Evaluating Celebrity Appeal

Did you know that there are actual "scores" to help you evaluate how appealing a particular celebrity is to the public? One useful tool is to find out a celebrity's Q Score (www.QScores.com). The Q Score is the industry standard for measuring the likability and familiarity of celebrities.

Here's how it works: Twice a year (in January and July), the Q Score Company measures more than 1,700 personalities. Each personality is rated by a national representative sample of 1,900 children, teens and adults. The question asked is:

In your opinion, indicate if the performer is:

1. One of my favorites

2. Very good

3. Good

4. Fair

5. Poor

6. Someone you've never heard of

You can purchase an individual report for one celebrity, or the entire report on all personalities.

Another source of information on celebrity appeal is available from Nielsen Media Research (ww.NielsenMedia.com). These are the same folks who track the Nielsen Ratings for television viewing. You can view and purchase a range of reports at the Nielsen Web site.

Don't despair if you can't afford the two options above, as they can be quite expensive. If you're willing to do the research yourself, here are some creative ways you can still get a good sense of which celebrity is best to tie in with your product or company:

Conduct an e-mail survey or poll your customers. I recommend WebPoll by Sparklit (webpoll.sparklit.com) for a simple poll, or SurveyMonkey (www.SurveyMonkey.com) for more complex surveys.

Keep the poll or survey simple, and offer an incentive for people to respond (a coupon, discount, etc.) Ask your customers to pick from a short list of celebrities you've already selected, or ask them to suggest names of celebrities using these two questions:

1. What celebrity could you most likely picture being in a commercial for this product?

2. Which celebrity would you most like to have dinner with to discuss this product?

If your product is aimed at a specific sex, such as with women's jewelry, specify "female celebrity" so your customers don't name male celebrities you wouldn't even consider. Go through the list and see how many names match both questions. This becomes the list of personalities you should pursue.

Use the Internet and bookstores to do research. For example, every year *Forbes* magazine publishes a list of stars called the "Celebrity 100" (www.forbes.com/celebrity100). The magazine compiles this list from ranking services and publications such as *Billboard*, *Pollstar*, Adams Media Research, Nielsen SoundScan and Nielsen BookScan. They also look at other metrics such as Web mentions on Google, press clips compiled by LexisNexis, TV and radio mentions by Factiva, the number of times a celebrity's face appeared on the cover of 26 major consumer magazines, and more. *Forbes* calls this evaluation the "E-Score," a "celebrity appeal ranking comprised of 46 separate personality attributes."

If it comes down to choosing between two celebrities and you can't decide which will be the most recognized, another tool you can use for evaluating celebrity appeal is Google Fight (www.GoogleFight.com). You simply enter in two search terms as you would on Google, and they "fight" to let you know which term has more listings on the Web. You can put in the names of two celebrities and see which is most popular on the Internet. This won't reveal the better choice for your product or company, but it will help you gauge popularity (online, at least).

If you're the CEO of a Fortune 500 company, you'll probably be able to afford bigger celebrities. I'm not saying you should, but you could. If you're operating a small business, however, superstars are probably not an option for you. But as I'll soon show you, there are many inexpensive ways to tie your product to a celebrity–even for free.

Let's pretend that you design fancy dog collars. You should go after stars who have a passion for dogs or animals in general. One way to find this out is to research the causes to which celebrities contribute. You can use the free Celebrity Causes Database (www.CelebCauses.com). For example, when I choose "animals" from the "All Causes" dropdown box, I get a list of 128 celebrities who are known to contribute to animal causes. Two of these stars are Betty White and Alicia Silverstone. Both are still famous, but not currently working as much as they used to.

They also have a passion for animals, so they're great ⌐ to approach.

Another option is to choose a star that isn't know⌐ lications such as the *Hollywood Reporter* (www.Hollyw⌐ and *Variety* (www.Variety.com) list actors who have just been cast in upcoming films but are not yet household names. For example, a couple of years ago, the *Hollywood Reporter* wrote about Brandon Routh being cast to play Superman. That would have been the perfect time to begin contacting him to see if he would be willing to endorse your product or somehow tie into your business, because he wasn't known yet but was about to become the next Superman.

This strategy is particularly useful because the trades are constantly writing about unknown performers who are being cast in major films and who will soon become stars. The articles usually even name the celebrity's agent and manager. If they don't, you can refer to Contact Any Celebrity's (www.ContactAnyCelebrity.com) online database of celebrity contact information including the agent, manager, publicist and production company with phone, fax and email addresses.

CHAPTER 4:

Getting Your Products in Celebrities' Hands

"Pop culture is the largest export in America. If you're
lucky enough to have access, you can win big."
Gene Simmons
KISS

Skeptics point out that when you give your product to celebrities for free (or "gift" them), there is no guarantee you'll get the publicity you're aiming for. However, this is true for most shots at free publicity. If you want guaranteed coverage, you'll have to advertise. But this doesn't give you the added benefit of an endorsement. In other words, everyone knows you are paying for the ad. The reality is that many entrepreneurs have made their businesses famous by giving celebrities their products.

In his book *Meatball Sundae*, marketing expert Seth Godin points out that one of the first merchants to gift celebrities—in his case royalty—was a potter named Josiah Wedgwood in the 1770s. Godin says, "He sent, without asking first, samples of his pottery to one thousand wealthy Germans. Believe it or not, more than half of them turned around and ordered more pottery. Several years before that,

Wedgwood gave Queen Charlotte (the wife of George III) a breakfast set. A few years later, she ordered a full tea service, which of course he turned into Queensware and sold to the masses. He also created bespoke china for Catherine the Great of Russia. Though he made little profit on the commission, his real profit was in displaying the finished works for months in London before shipping it off to Russia. That much-talked-about display attracted hordes of people to his showrooms. And many of those visitors turned into customers." Gifting royalty allowed Wedgwood to become the most successful potter of all time.

Success Story: Estee Lauder

"I don't know her very well, but she keeps sending me all these things."
- Princess Grace of Monaco about Estee Lauder

Princess Grace's quote touches on the practice Josiah Wedgwood started that still takes place today—gifting celebrities. Open any magazine and chances are you'll see a photograph of a star holding a spectacular handbag that's undoubtedly the "it" bag of the season. How did the celebrity get it? There's a good chance that she didn't buy it. Instead, the item was most likely given to the star in the hopes that she would love it and carry it with her to red carpet events or while being photographed by the paparazzi.

When first building her business, Estee Lauder (www.EsteeLauder.com) gifted celebrities to help create what is now a $5 billion cosmetics company. She did this by giving product samples to guests at fancy parties and sending them in the mail to celebrities and public figures (she also created the "gift with purchase" incentive that you see today in so many cosmetics commercials)

Today, Estee Lauder (whose brands also include Aveda, Clinique, MAC, Bumble and Bumble, Lab Series, Origins and Prescriptives) still uses celebrities. The company has created fragrances for Bobbi Brown, Daisy Fuentes, Donald Trump, Donna Karan, Kate Spade, Michael Kors, Diddy, and Tommy Hilfiger; and as of this writing, the company uses Gwyneth Paltrow and Elizabeth Hurley as spokespeople.

You can do this, too. You might not be able to create a fragrance. But you can send your product to celebrities in the mail. One thing you should be aware of is that since 9/11, it's now more difficult to send unsolicited packages to celebrities. Just because a package is returned to you doesn't mean the address isn't correct. It just means it was refused. However, most celebrities have more than one address, with managers and publicists more willing to receive items for their clients than talent agents who only care about bookings and may return your package for legal reasons.

A common myth is that you should always contact a celebrity through his or her agent. The reality is that the agent is only concerned with getting his or her client paid jobs, such as in movies or on television. They do not care about your product, and will often return it unopened for legal reasons. Why? In the past, agents have been sued by writers sending scripts and story ideas in the mail that were rejected, but that were similar to a movie or television show that came out soon after. So today, most agencies automatically return packages unopened unless they are submitted by a recognized agency or attorney. Only send items in the mail to the celebrity's manager or publicist--never to the agent!

Gifting Celebrities by Mail

The hardest part about gifting celebrities by mail is locating the star's best mailing address. But with services such as Contact Any Celebrity (www.ContactAnyCelebrity.com), the work is done for you. My service, for example, lists the best mailing address, agent, manager, publicist, production company and charitable cause for each celebrity, plus the phone, fax, and e-mail address for each star's representative.

Other online services provide celebrity contact information, but beware that most are not up to date and are not geared to business people. They also usually only provide you with an address, not the celebrity's agent, manager and publicist. Remember, you get what you pay for. Free sites simply don't have the resources to hire people to research, cross-check, and update information daily.

Another resource is the Screen Actors Guild (SAG), that has a free "Actors to Locate" telephone hotline available for finding the agent of an actor or actress:

Actors to Locate: 323-549-6737

However, SAG will only give you the agency name and phone number for up to three celebrities at a time, so if you want more you'll have to call back. Because it's a free service, the hold times are usually quite long and you have to pay long distance. Often, the celebrity's listing you're looking for will show up with "no contact information listed." This is why I recommend using a fast, accurate service like ContactAnyCelebrity.com.

After you've found the celebrity's best address, you want to make sure your letter or package stands out from all the others the celebrity receives. Here's how your correspondence usually makes its way to the celebrity. First it goes to the company's mailroom, where it's sorted by the mailroom staff. (Many famous entertainment executives started out working in the mailroom, including Michael Ovitz, Barry Diller and David Geffen). You can read more about how the mailroom has influenced the entertainment industry in David Rensin's *The Mailroom: Hollywood History from the Bottom Up.*

From there, it's delivered to the assistant of the celebrity's representative. This person usually sorts his boss' (the representative's) mail into A, B, and C piles. The C pile (junkmail) is immediately thrown away. The B pile is fan letters and autograph requests that are usually given or sent to the celebrity, but not always. Sometimes they are responded to by assistants with pre-signed photos, or are even discarded. The A pile is "special" correspondence that is to be immediately forwarded to the celebrity. This is the pile you want to be in.

You can also send your product to news anchors. Boston-based jewelry designer Jane Ciccone sent her necklace to Robin Roberts of ABC's *Good Morning America*, which she wore resulting in publicity in *Vanity Fair, InStyle,* and *Real Simple.* Nancy Grace of *CNN Headline News* has said that she often wears necklaces on the air that viewers send her in the mail.

How do you make sure your letter or package gets noticed? First and foremost, make it look professional. Even if you run your company from a kitchen table, make sure you type your letters and have them printed on professional letterhead. That immediately adds credibility to your request. Spell check, spell check, spell check! (Checking your grammar couldn't hurt, either).

It's also best to use Priority Mail or Federal Express to send your correspondence. FedEx has a delivery option called Express Saver that's much less expensive than overnight delivery but still has a better chance of getting past gatekeepers because it's in a FedEx envelope. UPS has a similar service, but I've found most people get the best results using FedEx. This is probably because most people in Hollywood think of

Success Story: Amy Peters of Amy Peters Studio

One of my clients, Amy Peters, is a jewelry designer and the owner of Amy Peters Studio (www.AmyPetersStudio.com). Amy wanted to get her inspirational jewelry designs into the hands of celebrities, so she sent samples in the mail. Here's what Amy told Bill Stoller, editor of the *Free Publicity Newsletter* (PublicityInsider.com):

"I send gift baskets filled with my jewelry to celebrities that I want to target. Ashley Scott recently wore one of my designs to the premiere of the new movie *2 Fast 2 Furious* the day after she received my box of goodies. After one of the *Survivor* contestants appeared in numerous magazines wearing my jewelry, I laminated copies of the article and hung them up in my trade show booth—increasing interest in my work for new retailers. The stores that already carried my designs were all mailed copies of the magazines with my jewelry circled, and a blowup of the design attached so they could place it near my jewelry displays to increase sales on a retail level."

But that's not all. Amy also sent her jewelry to the wardrobe departments of hit TV shows. Here's what she told me:

I use Contact Any Celebrity (www.ContactAnyCelebrity.com) to get my product into the hands of the hottest celebrities. So far I have received personal thank-you notes from Courteney Cox Arquette, Angela Bassett and Halle Berry— that was out of five gift baskets sent. My work has been included in the SAG Awards gift basket and also in one of the Oscar Awards post-show events. Because of this, my jewelry has appeared on some of the hottest celebrities in Hollywood. My work was also featured on the hit show *The OC.* The costume designer was thrilled with our work and used almost all of the designs we sent her. As a direct result of this product placement, we received contracts to supply our jewelry to Amazon.com's *The OC* Web site. I'm always recommending Contact Any Celebrity to other designers."

FedEx as delivering important business documents to high-end professionals, whereas they think of UPS delivering QVC packages to housewives in the suburbs. I'm just saying.

While it may be tempting to write a long letter so your request gets attention, that's not the best approach. Celebrities, representatives and their assistants are way too busy to spend time reading lengthy communications. Because you're asking a celebrity to do something, even if there's a benefit to him or her, you should be brief and direct. If you're making a request, such as for an endorsement or to try out your product, ask for it.

Decide what's most important to you. Don't ask for an autograph and then say you'd like the star to come to your store opening. Making your request the other way around can actually work to your advantage because of an important psychological principle called the Door in the Face technique:

Door in the Face Technique. Under this principle, when someone turns down a large request, they are more likely to comply with a smaller one. For example, if you're asking a celebrity to come to an event, that's a large request. So if you think the celebrity will probably say "no," also ask for a smaller request: "If you're unable to attend this event, please consider donating an autographed item for our silent auction."

Similarly, another principle known as the Foot in the Door Technique can also help:

Foot in the Door Technique. Under this principle, when someone first complies with a small request, they are more likely to later comply with a larger request. If you can get a celebrity to try out your product, you're more likely to get an endorsement later.

Keep your letter short and to the point while being enthusiastic yet sincere. Briefly introduce yourself and your business or product. Make sure to clearly state what you want. That is the number one mistake most people make—they ramble on, without clearly and succinctly stating their request.

Here's an example of a successful letter:

Dear Ms. Celebrity,

My business and I have a new pet carrier that would be perfect for you. I heard you speak on the XYZ Morning Show about how difficult it is for you to take your dogs with you when you go on tour. I too hated having to put my beloved terrier into a small, uncomfortable carrier.

I would like to send you a custom carrier that we've designed just for you. Because I'm a huge fan of yours, it's on the house! Please let me know if that would be acceptable and where I should send it. I will pay any necessary shipping and handling charges.

I look forward to your response.

Cordially,

[Your Signature]

[Your Name]
[Your Address]
[Your E-mail]
[Your Phone]

Celebrities like products that are made just for them. That's why I included the word "custom" in the letter above. If you have a way to customize your product–perhaps by engraving the celebrity's initials or adding some "bling" especially if it's a musician or athlete–this will help your products get noticed and appreciated.

Of course, make sure you include all of your relevant contact information along with your phone number, e-mail and mailing address. You should also include a self-addressed stamped envelope and perhaps a short form on which the person can specify the address where the product should be shipped, plus any special instructions. You don't know how the celebrity or the celebrity's assistant will want to contact you, so make it as easy as possible. They may call or send a quick e-mail.

Try to include a professional photograph of yourself using the product. Or even better, send photos of other celebrities using the product along with testimonials if you have any. Including this "social proof" is one way to distinguish your request from similar ones the star might receive.

Be patient. While you'll sometimes get lucky and receive a response almost immediately, it's more likely to take four to six weeks–although it could take much longer, and of course there's no guarantee you'll get a response at all.

While you're waiting, write to other celebrities. It's a numbers game. The more celebrities you write to, the better your chance of getting a response. If you haven't heard back, you can politely follow up after a few weeks to ask whether your inquiry was received or whether you can go ahead and send the product.

Success Story: Tracy Sanders, Wear Your Manners

Here's an example of an entrepreneur who sent her products to the right celebrities. Tracy Sanders of Wear Your Manners (www.WearYourManners.com) designs child-friendly T-shirts. She sent a bunch of her designs to celebrities who recently had children and received thank you notes from Doug Savant (*Desperate Housewives*) and his wife Laura Leighton (*Melrose Place*) as well as Elisabeth Hasselbeck (*The View*). Sanders then mentioned these responses on her Web site, brochures, press kits, and during media appearances.

First, she researched which celebrities had young children or were pregnant. Every time she saw these stars in celebrity magazines such as *Us Weekly* or *In Touch*, she would make a note. Celebrity magazines are valuable research tools. Start using them, and you may even be able to write off your subscriptions! Recently, a videographer asked me how he could find out the names of wedding planners who do celebrity weddings. A perusal of articles in these magazines about celebrities getting married turned up a mention of the wedding planner for almost every one. Then it was only a matter of Googling up the wedding planner's name online to find company contact information.

Here's what Tracy told me:

"I kept my letters short and sweet and to the point. I made sure to include all of my contact information and especially my e-mail address, because I knew the stars were so busy. I'm glad I did, because that's how I received the thank you notes. Most of them sent thank you notes back on their own. I thought that was really nice. I didn't ask for them. In fact, Elisabeth Hasselbeck from

The View wrote me about nine months later apologizing for the delay."

Here is an example of the letter Tracy sent:

Dear Mr. Savant,

I've been a huge fan of yours and would like to send you some T-shirts from my company Wear Your Manners.

Sincerely,

Tracy Sanders
Wear Your Manners
[Address]
[Phone]
[Email]

After receiving a thank you note from Doug Savant, Sanders e-mailed him and asked if she could quote him on her Web site, press kit, and in TV interviews. Savant wrote back and said, "Here's a quote we feel comfortable using." All he did was take out his children's names that he had originally mentioned. Here's the new quote he sent back:

Tracy,

Our whole family, even our teenager, loves your t-shirts! Our son regularly wears his "Don't hit" shirt to pre-school and others have noticed and commented on the shirt. We think you're onto something great, and support the positive messages your shirts send out into the world.

Continued success,

Doug Savant & Laura Leighton

Tracy can now say that stars of *Desperate Housewives, Melrose Place,* and *The View* have dressed their children in her t-shirt designs. You can do the same thing with your own products.

For more insider information on how to contact celebrities by mail, check out my book *Secrets to Contacting Celebrities and Public Figures: 101 Ways to Reach the Rich and Famous.* To get the best USPS-verified mailing addresses for more than 55,000 celebrities and public figures worldwide, check out my annual directory, *The Celebrity Black Book: Over 55,000 Accurate Celebrity Addresses for Fans, Businesses, Authors, Nonprofits, and the Media* (www.CelebrityBlackBook.com).

Approaching Celebrities in Person

Sometimes there's nothing like the personal touch—approaching a celebrity in person to make contact. If you want to get a photograph to put on your Web site (just being photographed with a celebrity will add to your credibility), find out where the celebrity will be appearing near you at book signings, charity and special events, trade shows and speaking engagements. Your local magazines and newspapers should fill you in. Another resource, *Autograph* magazine (www.AutographMagazine.com), lists where celebrities are appearing in cities across the country each month.

Success Story: Pauline Clifford of StarSparkles

Pauline Clifford took an innovative approach to getting her customized StarSparkles (www.StarSparkles.com) shoes into the hands of celebrities. So far her shoes have been worn by Paris Hilton, Britney Spears, Gwen Stefani, Kelly Osbourne and Scarlett Johansson, to name just a few. Pauline was even willing to travel from Europe to Los Angeles to get her product to celebrities in person—and her strategy worked.

JORDAN MCAULEY: How many stars did you gift your StarSparkles shoes to?

PAULINE CLIFFORD: I gave my shoes to about ten celebrities.

JM: How did you find the celebrities' contact information?

PC: I found their contact information using Contact Any Celebrity (www.ContactAnyCelebrity.com) and traveled from my home in Scotland to Los Angeles, where I have family. I handed most of my shoes to the celebrities' publicists or their receptionists. Some of the people were moody, but most of them were reasonably nice. I passed Paris Hilton's shoes on to someone in her manager's office. I had previously spoken to her manager, and he was one of the nicest people I spoke to.

JM: How did you find out that Paris Hilton wore your StarSparkles?

PC: When I returned home to Scotland, I found a photo of Paris wearing the shoes on a celebrity photo Web site. It's not only that she wore my StarSparkles, but how I went about it. People thought I was crazy spending all that time and money customizing the shoes, but I believed in myself and took the risk. Now people say that I have inspired them, and I find that really flattering.

JM: How has this helped your business?

PC: I used the fact that Paris Hilton wore my StarSparkles as publicity on my Web site. It also led to various newspaper and magazine articles. This has helped my business hugely!

JM: Have any other celebrities worn your shoes?

PC: I also StarSparkled shoes for Pharrell Williams, who was visiting Glasgow. I didn't get to meet him, but I did receive a nice, encouraging thank-you e-mail. I also customized shoes for Fergie of the Black Eyed Peas. After phoning her publicist's office, I was able to go backstage at a concert and give her the StarSparkles in person. Plus I got a photograph with her to put on my Web site.

JM: What tactics do you use to get to the stars?

PC: I don't think I have a particular tactic. If you're determined and pleasant, then sometimes people will give you a chance. If any celebrities come to Glasgow who I think would wear my StarSparkles, then I try to contact their manager or publicist. You can only try—the worst thing that can happen is nothing.

JM: Any other tips for getting products to celebrities in person?

PC: I've done a couple of freebie pairs of StarSparkles for the publicists and their assistants just to keep everyone happy. Also, check the Internet for photos of the celebrities wearing your product.

Have Celebrities Worn or Used Your Product?

Want to know if the item you sent to a celebrity was worn on the red carpet or seen elsewhere in their possession? Check these sites:

PerezHilton.com

X17Online.com

PRPhotos.com

WireImage.com

TMZ.com

For more insider information on how to contact celebrities in person, check out my book *Secrets to Contacting Celebrities and Public Figures: 101 Ways to Reach the Rich and Famous.*

What About Gift Certificates & Services?

Instead of giving actual products to celebrities, you can also send gift certificates for your business to celebrities in the mail, or place them in celebrity gift bags and gift suites. Another option is to demonstrate your service at celebrity events.

My client David McRae did this with his massage service, Tender Touch Massage (www.TenderTouchMassage.com). David says, "Last year, you placed an item in your Contact Any Celebrity Member Lounge looking for donations for gift bags that soap opera star Heather Tom could give out at a party at her house. I wrote and called her PR person and was able to do chair massages at the party for her and all of her soap opera star friends. That was a great opportunity."

Baeth Davis, better known as the Hand Analyst (www.HandAnalyst.com), promoted her new book, *Unleashing Your Purpose,* at an Emmy Awards gift suite and the Sundance Film Festival.

Baeth reads palms and wanted to include some celebrity handprints she could analyze in her book. By participating in the suite, Baeth was able to get handprints from *American Idol* judge Randy Jackson, Karina Smirnoff of *Dancing with the Stars*, Jean Smart of *Designing Women* and *Samantha Who?*, AnnaLynne McCord of *Nip/Tuck* and *90210*, and more.

My client Matthew Hunt, the founder of A Rose of Thanks (wwwARoseOfThanks.org), partners with churches and schools to send cards to troops overseas. To draw media attention, he gets celebrities to sign some of the cards at gift suites. He was able to get signed cards from Paula Abdul, *The Apprentice's* Omarosa, William Baldwin, *The Hills'* Audrina Patridge, and others.

Gifting Products to Celebrity Assistants

You've probably heard stories about the outlandish responsibilities that celebrity assistants have, and one is being a relentless gatekeeper. They also plan schedules, field phone calls, sort mail and open packages. That's why getting your product into the hands of a celebrity assistant can be as effective as reaching the celebrity.

The assistant is the one who tells the celebrity, "This is great—you have to try it!" And it's the assistant who's likely to respond when you send an e-mail or call to see if the celebrity is willing to provide a testimonial or endorsement.

Insider Interview: Anthony Zelig, President
New York Celebrity Assistants Association

In addition to being president of the New York Celebrity Assistants Association (www.NYCelebrityAssistants.org), Zelig is also the personal assistant and estate manager to David Koch, the second wealthiest resident in New York City and co-owner of Koch Industries, the largest privately held company in the U.S.

JORDAN MCAULEY: How do your meetings work?

ANTHONY ZELIG: We try to come up with a different theme each month that relates to our line of work. If a product ties into the meeting's theme, like a product that make our lives easier or our employer's (the celebrity's) life easier, representatives can come to the meeting and tell us about them.

JM: Tell us about your Unique Gifts meeting.

AZ: Once a year, we hold our annual Unique Gifts meeting to help the assistants prepare for the holiday season. This is our most popular meeting, where about a dozen vendors present to more than 75 celebrity assistants. We set up a big room with tables and go around talking to each vendor about the product they're showcasing. The meeting is geared toward us having an easier shopping time for our employers, because shopping for them during the holidays can get extremely busy and hectic.

JM: You also have some other opportunities, correct?

AZ: We do. Throughout the year we raffle off products and services to the assistants, like spa treatments. We also work with companies, vendors, and even locations to tie into our meetings. We try to get a nice variety of products for both males and females, usually a pet vendor, a toy company, artists, etc. We like to support smaller vendors as well. For example, we've had a glass blower and a pottery worker come to our meetings.

JM: What is the benefit of vendors pitching products to your assistants?

AZ: Vendors gift us with their products because they know that if we like something, we'll probably recommend it to our employer (the celebrity) or at least vouch for it. It also gives us a personal shopping contact at the business for help or ideas, because we have to work so quickly shopping for our employers. Sometimes our bosses can be very demanding, want things at the last minute, and/or want things that aren't necessarily available to everyone.

JM: How can people contact your association?

AZ: The best way to contact us is through our Web site at www.NYCelebrityAssistants.org.

For more details on when the next annual Unique Gifts meeting will be held in New York, contact:

New York Celebrity Assistants Association
459 Columbus Avenue, #216
New York, NY 10024
212-803-5444 (Phone)
www.NYCelebrityAssistants.org

There is also a Los Angeles and U.K. association:

Association of Celebrity Personal Assistants
914 Westwood Boulevard, #507
Los Angeles, CA 90024
www.CelebrityAssistants.org

Association of Celebrity Personal Assistants (UK)
206 Canalot Studios
222 Kensal Road
London W10 5BN
UNITED KINGDOM
www.ACA-UK.com

CHAPTER 5:

Getting Products in Celebrity Gift Bags

"Gift bags have become so de rigueur that stars of every caliber expect fabulous freebies to be handed out like candy at every Hollywood event."
USA Today

Celebrity gift bags are given to attendees, hosts and others at events ranging from award shows to movie premieres to charity functions. These products are usually selected by a company that specializes in putting together celebrity gift bags. Having your item selected can really boost your business, because if your item is included you'll be able to:

- Mention in media releases that your product was selected to be in the gift bags.

- Potentially have photos of your product appear on Web sites along with a link to where visitors can buy it.

- Get your product to celebrities who could be photographed using or wearing it.

- Have celebrities become future customers, ordering more products from you for themselves or friends.

- Have celebrities endorse your product or even become a spokesperson.

Many people enjoy hearing about which products were included in what gift bags. *Us Weekly* usually features articles about celebrity gift bags, mentioning products that were inside and where readers can enter contests to win bags from different events.

Karen Wood of Backstage Creations told *USA Today*, "At last month's Sundance Film Festival, there seemed to be a bigger focus on the swag than the films."

Insider Interview: Rebecca Lightsey, Gifted Presence

Rebecca Lightsey of Gifted Presence (www.GiftedPresence.net) is an expert on celebrity gift bags. Her service connects gift sources to celebrities and other influencers by creating the bags, sponsoring events, and more.

JORDAN MCAULEY: Do the gift bags usually only go to celebrities or to everyone who attends the event?

REBECCA LIGHTSEY: Ours only go to the celebrities, and then we usually do a giveaway with a radio station. Or, if the gift bag is related to a charity event, we do an auction with the proceeds going back to that organization.

JM: Are you open to all products or do you only look for big-name companies?

RL: As long as the product goes with the event, we're open to anything. For a recent father-daughter event, I was looking for men's and girl's products—anything for young children to women—because the daughters were all different ages. Obviously, if we're doing a sporting event, we wouldn't want to include cosmetics and items like that. We also always like to introduce new products.

JM: You also provide photos of products included in the bags to the media.

RL: We display all of the products on a table, so they aren't just stuck in a bag. Maybe there's only one necklace in each bag, but we put more than one on the table so the media can see the different styles. When celebrities come over to get their gift bag, we take pictures of them near the table picking up some of the items.

JM: Is the vendor then allowed to use the photos?

RL: They're allowed to use all the photos but not for any paid promotion like advertising. For example, if a jewelry designer had a picture of a star wearing her necklace, she could take it to retail stores where she wants to get her line into, or she could display it at trade shows. She could put the photo up on her Web site or in her brochures. But she couldn't use the photo in an ad in a magazine.

JM: How do you know if a celebrity likes your product?

RL: With your product, you can include a note that says, "We would love to provide jewelry for you in the future. If you ever need anything, please give us a call." Include your card and say what your product is, that it was in the gift bag at X event or something else that will jog their memory.

JM: Can you ask for feedback?

RL: We don't like to include a lot of promotional information because that's too sales-focused, but a note offering something in the future is definitely a good way to go.

JM: What should be included with the item?

RL: We definitely like the vendor to include a business card or some sort of contact information if it isn't already on the product's tag. That way, the celebrity can get in touch with you whether you provide a note or not. We did an event for the Golden Globes, and Marcia Cross from *Desperate Housewives* loved one of the jewelry items. She ended up calling the designer and buying jewelry for all of the guests at her baby shower.

JM: Any more tips on getting items in celebrity gift bags?

RL: There are all kinds of events you can do. Don't do just one event and then give up if you don't get the exposure you want. The better your product is suited for the event, the better chance you have of getting more exposure or having celebrities contact you because they really like your product.

JM: How many items does a company usually have to donate?

RL: It varies. I just did gift bags for a celebrity baseball game in Dallas. That one was 70 so all the players on the team could get a bag. We've also done very small events where we needed less than ten of the products.

JM: How can people find out about the events you have coming up?

RL: We have our Web site, GiftedPresence.net. We also work with PR companies, and I post celebrity gift bag opportunities in the Contact Any Celebrity (www.ContactAnyCelebrity.com) Member Lounge. I also keep a running list of people I've worked with and send them information on events I'm working on that they'll be particularly interested in.

Many businesses have leveraged their coverage from being included in celebrity gift bags to getting their products sold at mainstream stores. Sharps Barber & Shop (www.SharpsUSA.com), an all-natural lotion and soap line, was one of them.

The company's products were first included in celebrity gift bags at MTV events. Soon, stores such as Sephora and Fred Segal in Los Angeles began carrying them. Media coverage continued with magazines such as *Esquire*, *GQ*, and *InStyle* naming celebrities who used the soaps—Johnny Depp, Colin Farrell, and Justin Timberlake, among others.

Success Story: Phyllis Pometta of Baby Swags

Phyllis Pometta is the founder of Baby Swags (www.BabySwags.com), a company designed to promote baby products made by work-at-home moms.

JORDAN MCAULEY: Tell us about your business.

PHYLLIS POMETTA: We supply new celebrity moms and dads with Baby Swags gift baskets that are full of handcrafted, mom-inspired products. That is what makes Baby Swags unique—none of our products are mass-marketed.

JM: How do you contact the celebrities?

PP: From the moment I started my business in September 2006, I began using Contact Any Celebrity (www.ContactAnyCelebrity.com), and now I use it to make all of my contacts. The database is always on spot, which makes my job a lot easier. For instance, I sent out about 30 gift baskets during an 11-month period and had no returns, no wrong addresses, and have had great celebrity feedback.

JM: Do you also create gift baskets for events?

PP: We provide baskets for charity functions and silent auctions like the March of Dimes, and award shows like the Emmy Awards and Grammys. We also put together our very own "Baby Swags Emmy Basket" that was gifted to all the nominees in 12 categories.

JM: What results have you seen?

PP: All of my clients received a personal thank-you note from Jennie Garth, and I even got a phone call from Brooke Burke. It has truly been an amazing experience. We've also put together gift baskets for Jason Priestley, Julia Roberts, Salma Hayek, and more. You can see them all at: www.babyswags.com/whos_been_swagged.htm.

CHAPTER 6:

Getting Your Products in Celebrity Gift Suites

"Estée Lauder shrewdly vied for the approval of movie stars and royalty—people whom ordinary folk admired and looked up to. She understood that the endorsements of the rich and beautiful would give her products added believability for their high quality and value."

Mark Joyner
The Irresistible Offer
www.Simpleology.com

You've probably heard about the lavish "gift suites" stars visit right before major events such as the Oscars or Grammys. Usually in an upscale hotel, these suites are filled with products like clothing, accessories, gift certificates for spa treatments, vacations, and more.

Celebrities are happy to get the products for free, while the vendors get their products into the celebrities' hands, photos of their products with the celebrities, relationships with the stars, and other benefits. The media are usually invited into the gift suite as well, so the stars, the event, and the gift suite products also get press coverage. These suites are often shown on television programs such as *Access Hollywood* and *Entertainment Tonight*, with additional coverage in celebrity magazines.

Gift suites have been around about a decade. The first gift suite company, Backstage Creations (www.BackstageCreations.com), was started by Karen Wood, a former talent coordinator. Today, about a dozen companies organize gift suites, and these suites are more popular than ever. When the Golden Globe Awards was canceled in January 2008 due to the writers' strike, the gift suites went on as planned because the stars loved them so much.

I'm an advocate of getting free publicity whenever you can, but usually the only way to get your product included in a celebrity gift suite is to pay. These suites vary in price from $2,000 to $20,000, but the money is well-spent if you leverage the celebrity connections and publicity you receive.

When exhibiting at a gift suite, make sure to have your press kits with you, because you want to make sure reporters can take your information with them when the exhibit is over. The media will mostly focus on celebrities visiting the gift suites, but some reporters—especially those writing for print publications—will write follow-up articles on the products. Your press kit will be helpful to the writer.

The type of event will determine which items are featured. Obviously, the bigger the event—such as the Oscars or other award shows—the costlier the items. That's where expensive handbags or jewelry or the latest electronic gadgets are likely to be selected. But there's opportunity for less expensive selections as other events.

Insider Interview: Gavin Keilly, GBK Productions

Gavin Keilly of GBK Productions (www.GBKProductions.com) in Beverly Hills went from being director of development at the research hospital City of Hope in southern California to running one of the most respected and successful celebrity gifting suite companies.

I spoke with Gavin about how these suites work and how to get product included in them:

JORDAN MCAULEY: What are some major benefits to getting a product into a celebrity gift suite?

GAVIN KEILLY: First, there's the opportunity to actually speak to many celebrities and tell them about your products. After a vendor gives the celebrity the product he or she wants, they also get a photo of the star holding, using, or wearing it. The company can then use these photos in their press releases, on their Web site, in their marketing materials, and at their trade shows.

The final benefit is the press. Typically, with our gift suites, anywhere from 30 to 50 different media outlets come in, like *Us Weekly*, *In Touch*, *People Magazine*, *Extra*, *Access Hollywood*, *Entertainment Tonight*, and more. Businesses have the opportunity to speak to the press and get stories written about the company as well.

JM: Describe a typical celebrity gift suite and how it works.

GK: In a typical gift suite, there are probably 40 to 50 different vendors with a wide range of products available. There are expensive products like a $7,000 vacation to the Bahamas or a $10,000 watch, to inexpensive products like candles and makeup. With our gift suites, we also provide services like pedicures, manicures, facials, and massages to pamper the celebrities while they're there. We also have a bar, so the stars can come in and have a few cocktails.

Typically, we take over six to seven suites at a luxury hotel. For the MTV Movie Awards, for example, we were in the Presidential Suite at a hotel and the six suites attached to it. My staff actually walks the celebrity around to the vendors. Each one has the opportunity to speak to the celebrity and tell him or her about the product and then get a photo taken with the celebrity holding, using, or wearing it.

On average, celebrities spend about an hour and a half to two hours in our gift suites. I won't mention any names, but some celebrities have even spent six to seven hours! It's all about having a good time and creating a relaxing atmosphere for them.

JM: Do the celebrities know they are expected to pose with the products?

GK: Yes, they know that it's a quid-pro thing. Now, sometimes you'll have celebrities who say they're not willing to take any photos. In that situation, the vendor can decide whether or not to gift the celebrity. One celebrity in particular came to our gift suite and wanted to be gifted without taking photos, but we got a tremendous amount of press just by that big celebrity being there. We also got some quotes from him as far as loving certain products, so the vendor was happy.

JM: Are there rules for how many items a celebrity can get for free?

GK: The rule is that they can take one of anything they want from each vendor. An escort walks them around, and we have a lot of security. We also don't allow assistants to come into the gift suite. If someone says, "Tom Cruise asked me to come for him," we wouldn't allow that. The celebrity has to come directly to the suite to receive his or her items.

JM: How do businesses get their products into gift suites?

GK: We have almost a "first come, first served" type of thing, but of course, we're making the final judgment as to whether a product is appropriate or not. At the same time, we try to have exclusivity. If we have a jeans line, we'll only have one jeans company there. If we have a brand of men's shoes, we'll only have one brand of men's shoes. We always try to keep the categories exclusive.

JM: Are there any types of products you don't accept?

GK: I'd say always try, but if it's something terribly offensive, we probably wouldn't allow it. Still, there are also ways to do certain things. For example, we had Doc Johnson—an adult novelty company—that wanted to put their items in our gift suites. Instead of actually having them on display, we put them in elegant boxes.

JM: How much does it usually cost to get a product into a gift suite?

GK: It really depends on the event, but most of the award shows range from $5,000 to $15,000 to participate. However, for some of the smaller events, like a charity event with only 20 or 25 celebrities, it usually costs about $2,500.

JM: In addition to the fee, how many products need to be donated?

GK: For award shows it's about 70 and for charity events it's about 20 to 25.

JM: Are the products in gift suites all brand names?

GK: I'd say probably 70 percent of my clients are not brand names.

JM: That's good new for small businesses. What are some of the characteristics that you look for in a product?

GK: The two main factors are that it's unique and something the celebrities are going to like. One example of an item that was great, but I didn't think was going to get as good a response as it did, was a $25 toaster. When you put a piece of bread in it and hit "toast," a different character appeared on it depending on which template you used. The celebrities absolutely went berserk over it—loved it—and this was a $25 item. So you just never know.

JM: Does the product have to be new?

GK: No, we've had products that have been in the marketplace for 100 years. We had a wrinkle cream that has been around forever, that sort of thing.

JM: How are the products photographed with the celebrities?

GK: We do this differently than a lot of other companies who only have one or two photographers there. We have about seven or eight photographers in our gift suites to make sure we capture every "Kodak moment." Then our clients have the ability to get these photos within 24 hours so they can use them in their press releases and on their Web site. If the press requests photos, we provide them as well.

JM: Can celebrities sign the products?

GK: We allow vendors to have one of their posters or, let's say it's a surfboard company, have a surfboard there and have all of the celebrities sign the surfboard. Then the business can display the surfboard in their store or auction it off to benefit the charity of their choice.

JM: If a celebrity comes by and says, "I love this," can you use that celebrity's testimonial or do you have to get permission?

GK: You can use it. For example, Leonardo DiCaprio came into our last gift suite and loved that pop-up toaster. He said, "Oh my God, this toaster is phenomenal! My nephew would love it." That company is now using Leonardo DiCaprio's testimonial as "This toaster is phenomenal." He said it at the gift suite, so you can use it any way you want, so long as you quote him accurately.

JM: Do companies ever find spokespeople from having their products in a gift suite?

GK: It can happen. For example, there was a particular product in one of my gift suites. The first time this one particular celebrity took one, the vendor got a photo of the celebrity with the product. The celebrity went home, the vendor went home, and everyone was happy. The next time, the celebrity came in and said, "Oh my God, this cream is amazing; I remember you from last time, and it's fantastic. Can I get more of this? Can I also get it for my mom?" This time the vendor had the opportunity to talk to the celebrity further about the product and ask the celebrity to be a spokesperson. Sure enough, the celebrity is now doing commercials and all the other stuff.

DEALING WITH CELEBRITY GIFTING TAXES

Most people would agree that gift suites are a pretty good deal for both the stars visiting them and for the companies providing the products. However, as celebrity gifting became more and more elaborate with increasingly expensive products, the IRS began to pay attention. Their latest policy is that only gifts valued at more than $600 are taxable (to the celebrity, but not to the vendor). For now, however, there's not an effective way to enforce the regulation.

Gavin Keilly also notes that items in gift suites are usually unique products that aren't yet available in the marketplace. Because these are considered promotional items, they can't be taxed because there's no cash value attached to them.

Mindful of possible tax liability, some award shows have made changes to their gifting arrangements. The Hollywood Foreign Press Association, which paid back taxes on gift bags given out in prior years, gave presenters and audience members a more modest array of gifts valued at under $600 in 2007.

This is good news for small businesses and entrepreneurs, as many brand-name companies with products valued at thousands of dollars have stopped including their products in celebrity gift bags and suites because of the tax liabilities. Because yours is probably valued at under $600, you now have a better chance of having your product included.

The tax issue will probably continue to be debated for some time, with some stars willing to take as much as possible and others taking the gifts but donating them to charity. One year, George Clooney auctioned off his Oscar Good Bag online and donated the proceeds to United Way to help the victims of Hurricane Katrina.

CHAPTER 7:

Product Placement

"It is celebrity that transforms ordinary vodka into Trump vodka, bottled spring water into Trump Ice, and glassy high-rises into symbols of gilded, big-city aspiration. It is celebrity status that helps drive condominiums in Trump buildings to sell at a premium."

Secrets of the Super Rich,
U.S. News & World Report Special Edition

Almost as important to our culture as celebrities are the products they use and endorse. From BMW in *James Bond* to Coca-Cola on *American Idol*, product placement is a widely accepted practice in Hollywood and beyond. It's no longer taboo to show a specific product with its label facing forward on television, the big screen, or even at live concerts.

Marketers know millions of people around the world will see a particular product multiple times—for example, when a film is viewed in movie theaters, on DVD, and in trailers and previews. They may also hear about it in songs by their favorite musicians and see it on their favorite TV shows. Paid product placement also allows film studios, record labels, and television networks to recoup some of the lost costs to fans who download, burn, and share movies, music, and TV show.

According to the *Hollywood Reporter*, product placement showed up in the press for the first time with Reese's Pieces in 1982's *E.T.: The Extra-Terrestrial*. Before that movie, product placement was referred to as "exploitation," "hidden plugs" or "product plugs," according to the magazine. The turning point came in 1995 with James Bond's *GoldenEye*, when BMW spent $3 million on product promotion in the film.

Here are some other interesting moments in product history:

- In 1934, sales of men's undershirts plummeted after Clark Gable was shown bare-chested in *It Happened One Night*.
- In 1955, sales of Ace combs dramatically increased after James Dean was shown using one.
- In 1983, Tom Cruise made RayBan sunglasses extremely popular when he wore them in *Risky Business*.

Paid product placement has significantly increased not just in the United States but overseas as well. The American Marketing Association (www.MarketingPower.com) even offers an online course on Movie and TV Product Placement with contributions from professors at major universities. Some $2.9 billion was spent on product placement alone in 2007, according to the research consulting company PQ Media (www.PQMedia.com).

Recently Bravo, the television network famous for hit reality shows like Top Chef, The Real Housewives, Millionaire Matchmaker, and the Rachel Zoe Project, began advertising 1B product placement opportunities with full-age ads in the New York Times and on billboards in New York City. Visit Affluencers.com to learn more.

TiVo has played a large part in the rise of product placement. As more and more people began skipping commercials, sponsors have begun weaving products directly into shows so they're impossible to miss. Peter Berg, producer of television series such as *Friday Night Lights*, told *USA Today* that product placement is about "giving [the audience] what they need in a way that doesn't violate the integrity or offend the audience to feel like they're being subliminally manipulated into watching a commercial."

In a unique development for product placement, some Web sites allow consumers to search for products they see their favorite stars wearing and using on television shows and in movies.

These Web sites include:

Seen On - www.SeenOn.com

CW Style - www.cwtv.com/thecw/style

StarStyle - www.StarStyle.com

What Celebs Wear - www.WhatCelebsWear.com

If you're like most small businesses, you don't have a huge marketing budget to spend on product placement. Don't worry. While the Coca-Colas and BMWs of the world are spending hundreds of thousands of dollars buying product placement, you can get your products featured on the very same programs as a "trade out" (when a product is included without payment).

In the pages that follow, I'll reveal several "secret" strategies for getting your products placed on major TV shows and in blockbuster movies right along with the big guys— for *free* (except for shipping your product to the set).

Get Product Placement—Free!

It's a little-known fact that movie and television producers are constantly looking for ways to stay under budget by reducing expenses. This makes them look good to their bosses by staying under budget, and allows them to spend more on A-list talent. You may think that money is no object for movie and television studios, but that's not true. Producers are constantly watching expenses and trying to keep them from spiraling out of control due to unforeseen circumstances such as weather, late or sick actors, union strikes, etc.

Set decorators, craft services and wardrobe designers also don't want to spend time and money shopping for items when they can get them donated. Donated items also give productions a more realistic effect. Think about it. When was the last time you saw your favorite actor wearing a T-shirt with GAP emblazoned across the front of it on TV? Wardrobe items cannot be recognizable, and every character usually has to be in a different outfit in each scene and on every episode. That's a pain for the stylist and the wardrobe designer.

The same goes for home decor items and accessories. The producer doesn't want to go purchase a beautiful cake for a birthday party scene, or flowers for a wedding or funeral. If these items are donated, the producer saves money and the production feels more realistic.

Craft services work the same way. Movie and TV sets must constantly have a wide variety of food available to feed the talent and crew. One of the basic rules on any set is to keep the actors happy, because unhappy actors cost time—and as we all know, time is money. Cranky actors and actresses who storm off sets because they're tired or hungry do not a happy producer make.

Shoots often last long hours over several months or even years for TV shows. The actors and crew get tired of eating the same food, so craft services are constantly struggling to provide something new and different. If you own a restaurant, bakery, or any food or beverage company, odds are you can donate product to the set in exchange for screen time and a credit. Imagine being able to tell your customers that your wedding cakes were featured on *Desperate Housewives* or your jewelry was worn on *Ugly Betty*. That's the marketing power of getting free product placement.

Scout Out Opportunities

So, how do you find out about these free product placement opportunities?

When watching a TV show you like, look for the name of the production company or producer. Then go online and search for the company's Web site to get the address. You can also call the television network and ask for the phone number of the program's production company. An even easier resource for finding out this information is the *Hollywood Creative Directory* (www.HCDOnline.com), a quarterly directory that lists television show staff members along with their contact information.

Simply contact the producer by mail and briefly ask if he or she has a need for your product. Explain why you think the show might want to use it. Don't write a long fan letter. Your goal is to simply introduce your product and let the producer know that you're available if there's a need—now or in the future.

Include a media kit that has photographs of your product with people using it as well as product dimensions, specs, and all your contact information. That way, the producers can keep it on file. Sometimes sending a product sample is the only way for the producer to see it firsthand and make a decision. Unfortunately, unsolicited packages are often returned unopened to the sender, so wait to send a sample until the producer has specifically asked for one.

This isn't the time to sit back and wait for your product to be selected. Reach out to several production companies at the same time. You don't know which producer will be interested in your product or how long it will take for it to be selected. There's no reason to have your heart set on one particular program, so approach several companies at once.

Also, check with your city and state Department of Film and Television Production. You should let the Film Commission know that you're willing to donate your products to any upcoming film productions. Also, if you think your store, restaurant, or even office could be used for filming, let the Film Commission know that as well.

Insider Expert: Amy Stumpf, Spotlight Branding

Amy Stumpf's Spotlight Branding (www.MySpotlightBranding.com) connects small businesses with openings for free product placement. Her service provides a constantly updated online database where you can search opportunities to donate your product in exchange for screen time.

JORDAN MCAULEY: How does your company find out about these free product placement opportunities?

AMY STUMPF: We talk with people on the set—the wardrobe designer, the prop master, the producers. When they need something, they need it immediately—not tomorrow. They're only planning two or three episodes ahead, so we're constantly in touch with them on a weekly basis to get the next batch of opportunities up in our system.

JM: Why do the production companies work with you?

AS: A lot of productions don't have a paid production resources coordinator on staff. It's a position that's been around but has changed titles from "product placement coordinator" to "production resources." Producers now realize that this is a great way to save money and add a level of reality to their sets, because they're not using the same stuff available at all the prop houses. They're getting free stuff, and the set doesn't look generic.

JM: How do you pitch a product for television coverage?

AS: When you pitch products for television, you need to say, for example, Eva Longoria's character needs to wear this item for a particular reason on *Desperate Housewives*, and that it's a perfect fit for the show. You want to specifically mention the character and an attribute of the character. The more you know about the TV show or character you're pitching, the better.

Success Story: Amy Peters, Amy Peters Studio

Designer Amy Peters (www.AmyPetersStudio.com), who you met in the chapter on Gifting Celebrities, didn't just stop at sending her inspirational jewelry to celebrities in the mail. She also sent it to the wardrobe department of hit television shows with young, hip characters (her target market). One of these shows was Fox's hit teen drama *The O.C.* Amy received free product placement when the wardrobe designer outfitted several of the characters on the show with the jewelry she sent.

CHAPTER 8

Holding Celebrity-Themed Events

*"One of the biggest issues most marketers have is being BORING!
Zzzzzzzzzz... You want your customers and prospects to be thinking,
'Wow! What's this crazy guy (or gal) going to do next?"*

Yanik Silver, Founder
Maverick Business Adventures
www.MaverickBusinessAdventures.com

Instead of just holding another event, why not hold a celebrity-themed or Hollywood-themed event? Hire a celebrity to speak and then sign autographs and take photos with your customers, and you'll be one step closer to getting people to spread the word about your business.

Hollywood, Here We Come!

Why not hold your celebrity-themed event in Hollywood so the location goes along with your theme? Many movie studios offer event planners and facilities, plus you can entertain guests with a studio tour before or after the event. And they may even spot some celebrities while they're there!

Here are a few movie studios that host events:

PARAMOUNT PICTURES

5555 Melrose Avenue

Hollywood, CA 90038

323-956-8398 (Phone)

www.Paramount.com

Situated on 63 acres, Paramount Studios is the oldest working movie studio left. It has a variety of venues on the lot, including the famous New York back lot that can hold up to 500 people. Your guests can also go on a behind-the-scenes tour of the studio. I attended an alumni event that my university held there once—and from my experience, I can assure you that your attendees will love it.

WARNER BROS. STUDIO

4000 Warner Boulevard

Building 225

Burbank, CA 91522

818-954-2652 (Phone)

www.WBSpecialEvents.com

Warner Bros. has just started hosting theme events. You can hold yours at the studio or at a location of your choice. Warner Bros. offers back-lot streets, private screening rooms, and even a jungle.

NBC UNIVERSAL SPECIAL EVENTS

100 Universal City Plaza

Universal City, CA 91809

818-777-9466 (Phone)

www.nbcuni.com/studio

Universal Studios offers a back-lot movie set, a historical sound stage, and a world-famous studio restaurant, and also offers event venues at the New York City location.

Here are some other places perfect for holding a celebrity-themed event:

THE PLAYBOY MANSION

For a racier event, how about renting the Playboy Mansion? (It's now popular with both men and women because of the hit E! television series *The Girls Next Door* and the movie *The House Bunny*). Internet marketing consultant "The Rich Jerk" (www.PartyWithRichJerk.com) has rented out the Playboy Mansion for many customer appreciation events. When you hold an event at a venue like this, many people will pay more just to be able to go (especially guys!). Think about a space that will add value and also allow you to charge more because people will want to be there.

Playboy Mansion
10236 Charing Cross Road
Los Angeles, CA 90024
www.PartyWithTheBunnies.com

STUDIO 54

If you're on the East Coast, you can rent out the Roundabout Theatre Company for your celebrity-themed event, better known in the late 1970s as the world-famous Studio 54 nightclub.

Roundabout Theatre Company
254 W. 54th Street
New York, NY 10019
212-719-9393 (Phone)
www.RoundaboutTheatre.org

Insider Expert: Yanik Silver

Internet marketing expert Yanik Silver (www.YanikSilver.com) frequently holds seminars and customer appreciation events centered on a Hollywood spy theme. His Underground™ Online Seminars (www.UndergroundOnlineSeminar.com) have become extremely popular because of all the underground Internet marketing secrets he reveals—and because of all his clever tie-ins to popular celebrities, television shows and movies.

For one of his first events, the Underground™ Online Seminar I, Yanik created a mixed-bag spy theme with a VIP party at a spy museum. He also held a contest where Yanik gave away a two-day "Ultimate Mission Impossible" experience by booking a trip with Incredible Adventures (www.Incredible-Adventures.com). The lucky winner got to take part in a live hostage rescue operation, drive like James Bond, and receive weapons training with Green Beret and Delta Force instructors.

At his next Underground gathering, Yanik tied into celebrities even more with an *Austin Powers*-inspired event complete with roller girls, a VIP party, and a live appearance by Verne Troyer (Mini-Me in the *Austin Powers* movies) with photo and autograph opportunities. He even gave away a Mini Cooper "getaway spy car."

Yanik says, "Surprisingly, it's not as much as you'd think to book a celebrity [depending on their status], and it can really add a lot to your events. Having a celebrity not only gives your guests excitement but provides additional reasons to contact your customers. For example, I sent a personalized postcard out to my list announcing Verne Troyer was coming. The front of the postcard had Mini-Me's picture with the words '[First Name], Can't Wait to Meet You!' and Verne's autographed signature at the bottom."

And Yanik kept going. His next two events continued along the celebrity/spy theme. For the U.S. version, Yanik hired actor Peter Graves from the original *Mission Impossible* television series to appear. The U.K. event had a *James Bond* theme.

Yanik says, "One of the biggest issues most marketers have is being BORING! Zzzzzzzzzz... You want your customers and prospects to be thinking, 'Wow! What's this crazy guy (or gal) going to do next?' It's no secret that the majority of your customers or prospects live somewhat boring lives. So it's not enough anymore just to present an offer filled with benefits—it's also got to entertain them and keep it exciting."

Hiring an Event Photographer

For special events, parties, openings, seminars, etc., you'll want to hire a professional photographer. Make sure that he or she regularly shoots special events. Also, make sure that they'll be taking digital photos at a high-enough resolution for magazines. Most do these days, but check just to make sure. Let the photographer know you want to have unlimited usage rights to these photos, and get something in writing. If you don't, the photographer legally owns the copyright and can technically bar you from using his photos in your marketing materials (Web site, brochures, sales letters, etc.)

For a book release party I produced, I hired a freelance photographer who was very good...at getting shots of me and my co-author. That was great, but he hardly got any photos of the other guests who attended. Besides the regular guests, he should have also taken photos of the various celebrities who attended, including a member of the country group Sugarland, a Georgia state representative, and several other well-known local celebrities.

After that experience, I've made sure that the photographer gets a few photos of me but also focuses on other guests—especially the celebrities. This is common sense, but both you and the photographer can forget during the excitement of an event in full swing.

When hiring an event photographer, it's best to get a referral from someone who was pleased with the photographer's earlier work. Call a few restaurants, clubs, etc., who have recently held high-end events, and ask whom they used. There's a lot more to being a good event photographer than simply running around a party snapping photos of guests holding martinis.

Getting good-quality, high-resolution photos that come out sharp and in focus is more difficult than it looks, especially at dimly lit events. If a celebrity performs, you'll want photos of that. This is an entirely different ball game because the photographer has to deal with the performer's movements, the stage lighting, the audience, etc.

It's best to hire a professional event photographer from a photo agency such as WireImage (www.WireImage.com) or Getty Images (www.GettyImages.com). One advantage of using a photo agency is that it will also syndicate your photos to the media (especially if the photographer gets good photos of celebrities at your event). The Patrick McMullan Co. (www.PatrickMcMullan.com) shoots 50 events per week, then syndicates the images to leading local, national and international publications. That can be great added publicity, especially if a photo from your event gets picked up in a magazine or newspaper.

Making the Most of Photo Opportunities

Try to get photos of your celebrity guests holding your product or at least walking around with it (non-posed is best so that it looks like a candid shot). If the celebrities don't want to do a non-posed photo, ask if they'll pose with you or with another key person from your company holding your product.

Scoopt (www.Scoopt.com) is owned and operated by Getty Images (www.GettyImages.com). Getty Images supplies photos around the clock to thousands of media companies worldwide including newspapers, magazines and broadcasters. Scoopt lets you join in as a citizen journalist by taking photos on your digital camera or cell phone, uploading them to the service for free, and getting paid a 40 percent royalty if a news outlet purchases the rights to use your photo.

CNN has gotten into the game as well, with a new online feature called iReport (www.cnn.com/ireport). This site allows you to post whatever news or information you choose, including photos and videos. Imagine the possibilities: You snap photos of celebrities attending your special event or store, restaurant, or club opening. You get celebrities to hold your product while you politely and quickly snap the images. Then you upload the photos to Scoopt or iReport.

"Seen At" Your Event

Many magazines (especially local ones and those that cover celebrities) have "Seen At" sections. These are usually a page or multiple pages with a collage of photos of various people at events, from regular people, to VIPs, to local and national celebrities.

As soon as you receive the high-resolution images from your event photographer, burn them to CD and send them to the photo editor at these publications. You can find out who the photo editor is simply by looking at the masthead of credits in the magazine or on the publication's Web site. Include a letter welcoming the editor to use the photos in an upcoming issue. Number each photo, and in your letter list the names of the guests along with the corresponding photo number. "Seen At" sections usually have captions under the photos, so you'll want to make sure your guests' names are correct.

If the photo editor runs the photos, your guests will be flattered that they're in a magazine, and you and your company will get free exposure (magazine advertising is expensive). Be sure to add your business or product name onto the event in your letter so the magazine will say something like "Seen At [Your Company]'s Launch Party."

Every time I've done this, the editor has actually thanked me for the photos because it costs them time and money to go out and photograph events, and they can't possibly cover all of them. By using your own photographer and sending the photos to magazine editors yourself, you're in control of the photos that might run.

CHAPTER 9:

Hiring Celebrities for Your Event

"When we added the glamour of celebrity names to our roster, attendance skyrocketed."

Bill Zanker, Founder
The Learning Annex

One of the ways celebrities earn extra money when they're not working on film, television or music projects is by appearing at or hosting special events. These usually include openings, nightclub parties, trade show and seminar appearances, etc.

Insider Interview: Craig Hirschfeld

Craig Hirschfeld (www.HowToHireACelebrity.com) is an event planner who has lined up celebrities from Joan Rivers to Tony Bennett to the Pointer Sisters for events in New York City. I asked Craig for his advice on working with booking agents.

JORDAN MCAULEY: What is the difference between a booking agent and a talent agent?

CRAIG HIRSCHFELD: A booking agent is like a middleman. They help you plan the event, select a site, and review contracts. They look out for the client's interest. You hire a booking agent to contact the celebrity through their agent or manager to get the best possible price. A booking agent handles everything that you may not know about.

JM: What are some of the benefits of using a booking agent?

CH: Booking agents have experience and helpful tips that will help save you money and make sure your event goes smoothly. Many times, agents or managers will recommend you to a particular booking agent. They may say, "We don't like to deal with so-and-so Joe Smith, but let me give you the name of a booking agent to contact." If they have experience, the booking agent also knows what celebrities work well for what types of events.

POINTS TO COVER WITH A BOOKING AGENT

When you talk with a booking agent, Craig Hirschfeld recommends that you discuss:

- The kind of event you're having.
- Your budget.
- What kind of talent is best for your event.

Points to Cover Regarding Your Audience

During the discussion with your booking agent, he or she should want to know the following about the expected attendees:

- How many people you expect.
- The breakdown of the audience (estimated percentage by age, gender, etc.).
- The audience's ethnicity.

The booking agent hears that you want X-celebrity to perform at your party. However, they may have used that person for another event and therefore knows that he or she isn't very easy to work with. A good booking agent has insider tips that can help with your event. I definitely recommend going through a booking agent as opposed to calling the talent agent directly.

Another benefit of using a booking agent is they're usually nonexclusive and have free range to anyone. If you call a talent agent directly, they'll try to sell you only the specific talent they represent. A good booking agent has relationships with many talent agencies and knows who's good for what event and can get you anyone you want.

The booking agent also knows what the approximate price should be for hiring the celebrity. They can say, "So-and-so paid X amount for this same type of event, why are you trying to charge me Y?" So they can negotiate and get you the best rate.

JM: Why is it important to get the demographics of those expected to attend the event?

CH: Try to get as much information as possible to suit the talent to the event. Especially with a comedian, not everyone is going to have the same taste. The booker should try to match up a celebrity who is going to be entertaining for your specific group.

Bookers and celebrities don't want your event to be bad because it makes both the booker and the talent look bad. If you hire a comedian and no one laughs, that doesn't make anyone look good. It's always important for the booker to ask key questions. Based on the answers, both of you can find a celebrity that's going to be great for that audience.

JM: What are some tips for doing a meet-and-greet or a photo opportunity?

CH: Many celebrities don't want to do a meet-and-greet. So if you want this, it's important to get a celebrity who is willing to do it, and make sure you get it in writing. You need to be specific in these contracts, like a meet-and-greet with pictures for 20 minutes. You also need to be even more specific and note whether it's going to be before or after the show, which is determined by the entertainer, not the client.

Some celebrities get very nervous no matter how many years they've been performing. Many don't want to see anyone before the event. They may agree to do a 20-minute meet-and-greet after the event. But if you don't have this in writing, the celebrity may change his or her mind after the show and say, "I'm tired, I'm out of here," or "I didn't like the audience, I'm leaving." So it's essential that you get everything in writing.

JM: What's the most important first step before hiring a celebrity?

CH: The first question you have to ask is, "What is the budget?" You could have a comedian who costs $500 or $1,500 as opposed to a singer at $250,000. The budget is always the first and most important question, then move into more specifics. What type of event is it? If it's for a nonprofit charity event, what is the charity? Is it geared to kids? If so, you want a celebrity who is child-friendly. You don't want to a hire a celebrity who is going to use foul language, for instance.

JM: What are some tips for working with the celebrities?

CH: For the most part, if you give them what they want, they're usually very nice and accommodating. No one wants to be difficult because they want to work again. Every once in a while, you'll get a celebrity who's a little demanding. But usually it's easy, as long as you follow what they want in the rider you should get from the booker prior to the event.

JM: **What is a rider exactly?**

CH: Basically it says everything the celebrity demands. It goes into detail about everything the celebrity needs in order to go on, in addition to items that people they are traveling with might need.

JM: **What are some ways to save money when hiring a celebrity?**

CH: You can negotiate the details ahead of time to limit your expenses. If a certain celebrity is already going to be in your area, you're obviously not going to want to pay air fare. You may not have to pay for their hotel, either. Sometimes you can go in with another business and split the cost of paying for the transportation and hotel. For instance, the celebrity could appear at your trade show booth and sign autographs in the afternoon, and then perform at another business' event in the evening.

JM: **Talk a little about choosing a good venue.**

CH: The venue is one of the most important factors in determining the kind of talent you want. Some places have great stages and are easy to work with because they do events all the time. A good booking agent will talk to the venue's manager and work out all the requirements ahead of time. Picking a venue that's friendly to performers is very important. You don't want to select a venue that has never hosted talent before or isn't capable of handling the talent.

JM: **If a celebrity is performing, how long should the performance last?**

CH: It should never last more than an hour because you'll lose the audience's interest. You always want to leave your audience wanting more, wondering, "What are they going to do next time?"—or leave your competitors thinking, "How are we ever going to top this event?"

It's Not the Size That Matters

Usually, it's unrealistic for most businesses to spend megabucks for a big-name celebrity. Instead, consider television actors, soap opera stars, reality TV stars, Playboy Playmates, standup comedians, etc. Reality TV stars are a great match for many events. Past contestants from shows like *The Apprentice* and *American Idol* are affordable and work well at corporate events. Cast members from reality shows like *The Real World* and *The Hills* are also affordable and make a great match for nightclubs or other teen/young adult events.

If it comes down to choosing between a big star who isn't willing to do a meet-and-greet with photos or a lesser-known star who is, I recommend choosing the smaller star. One of the most important things you want are photos of the celebrity attending your event so you can use them for your Web site, brochure, press kit, etc. You'll have a bigger impact with good photos of a smaller star than with a huge star who shows up for an hour but doesn't leave you with anything you can leverage.

Celebrity Alternatives

A fun alternative that works at most events is to hire a celebrity look-alike. I spoke on two panels at Internet marketing expert Corey Rudl's (www.CoreyRudlPresents.com) "Wedding Seminar" right before he passed away. Corey and his Internet Marketing Center (www.MarketingTips.com) had promised a big celebrity speaker in his promotion of the event. The celebrities ended up being George and Laura Bush impersonators. At first, I thought everyone might want their money back, but it went over surprisingly well. The "president" and "first lady" made a tongue-in-cheek speech during dinner and took photos with attendees. The crowd loved it, and it probably cost Corey very little.

Celebrity Impersonator Resources

Celebrity Impersonators
www.CelebrityImpersonators.com

Carbon Copies Celebrity Look-Alikes
www.CarbonCopiesCelebs.com

Darin Thrasher
(Elvis Presley)
www.ElvisThrasher.com

Melody Knighton
(Lucille Ball, Joan Crawford, Marlene Dietrich, Dolly Parton)
www.MelodyKnighton.com

Tapley Entertainment
www.LookALike.com

Another fun idea is to tie your event into a live or silent celebrity autograph auction with memorabilia from the celebrity who is appearing. Get him or her to donate some autographed items as part of your contract, or purchase some photos, posters, etc., and have the celebrity sign them at the event in front of everyone. Be sure to specify this in your contract, and get the items in advance.

To learn how to hold a celebrity autograph auction, check out my resource, *Help from Hollywood* (www.HelpFromHollywood.com).

Insider Interview: Mike Esterman, Esterman Entertainment

Mike Esterman of Esterman Entertainment (www.Esterman.com) is a celebrity "personal appearance agent" who books celebrities for private parties and events. He's been featured on the *Today Show*, E! Entertainment Television, *Inside Edition*, and CNN's *Showbiz Tonight* as a guest expert on celebrity events.

I spoke with Mike Esterman about how businesses can hire celebrities to help supercharge their marketing and publicity efforts.

JORDAN MCAULEY: Why should someone go through a celebrity booker like yourself as opposed to the celebrity's talent agent?

MIKE ESTERMAN: Because I actually answer the phone and will give you a quick answer. Sometimes you can't get the celebrity's talent agent on the phone.

JM: How far ahead should someone begin planning to book a celebrity?

ME: I have people calling me today needing a celebrity for tonight up until a few weeks or a few months from now.

JM: How much should someone expect to pay to book a celebrity?

ME: The price can range anywhere from $500 for a Playboy model or a reality TV star to $1.7 million for a private Justin Timberlake concert I was just asked about. It's a pretty wide range.

JM: What are some tips for saving money when booking a celebrity?

ME: One tip is if the celebrity is already going to be in your area, that's a good way to save money on travel because you don't have to pay for it. For example, many of the MTV *Real World* kids travel around the country speaking at colleges and like to pick up nightclub appearances as well. So you can save money that way. Or a musician who's already performing a concert on Thursday may want to pick up an appearance on Friday. Then you don't have to pay air fare, just another hotel room night.

Now I don't always know who's going to be in what area. People call me and ask if so and so is going to be in their area. I don't know that, although I list the ones I do know about on my Web site at www.Esterman.com. So if you know someone is going to be nearby, tell me. It's up to you to let me know so I can help save you money on travel.

JM: How does someone book a celebrity with you?

ME: My Web site (www.Esterman.com) is like a McDonald's menu of who's available. I can go after pretty much any celebrity and make them an offer, but the ones who are listed on my Web site are actively looking to book these types of arrangements. It's basically a three-step system: You choose a celebrity from my Web site, tell me how much you're willing to spend, and e-mail me the name. Then I make an offer to the celebrity. If the person is available, I draw up a contract and you put down a deposit. It's that easy.

JM: What kinds of business events will celebrities do?

ME: The corporate market is huge, and everybody wants to get a celebrity. I booked Carmen Electra to work an electronic company's trade show booth. Cindy Margolis hosted a Tupperware-like party where women came to buy purses. Jenna Jameson hosts nightclub parties for lingerie companies. In addition to trade shows and seminars, you can hire them for store and restaurant openings as well.

Shhh... Secret Celebrity Parties!

Deep in the heart of Hollywood lies a secret society of celebrity parties called Xenii. Xenii calls itself an "invitation-only membership community similar to a high-end mobile country club that uniquely combines the Great Gatsby era, the ingenuity of Andy Warhol's Factory, and the energy of Studio 54." It counts Cameron Diaz, Diddy, Jamie Foxx, Enrique Iglesias, Paris Hilton and Naomi Campbell among its members. Parties are open to Xenii members only and are hosted at secret locations throughout Los Angeles. The location changes every week, as does its unique theme.

The bad news—in case you haven't guessed—is that you have to be a celebrity to get invited to the party. The good news is that Xenii also owns an event production service that produces high-end parties for businesses and corporations. They've planned more than 100 events since 1995, so if you're looking to plan a high-end party complete with A-list celebrities, Xenii may be your answer.

Xenii
8228 W. Sunset Boulevard
West Hollywood, CA 90046
323-848-7888 (Phone)
323-848-9088 (Fax)
www.Xenii.com

Using Celebrity Wranglers

Do you simply want celebrities to show up at your event as guests, and not perform or host? If so, you may want to use a celebrity "wrangler" to make the invitations and arrangements. Celebrity wranglers are the go-to people when you want celebrities to show up at your event just as the public would. Wranglers have a network of celebrities they can invite to all types of events. You pay the wrangler either a flat fee or a per-celebrity rate that varies depending on your needs.

Insider Interview: Rita Tateel

I spoke with celebrity wrangler Rita Tateel of the Celebrity Source (CelebritySource.com) about hosting celebrities at your event. Rita has worked with Muhammad Ali, President George Bush, Bill Cosby, Gloria Estefan, Diana Ross, Wayne Gretzky, Magic Johnson, Jay Leno, George Lucas, Arnold Schwarzenegger, Gen. H. Norman Schwarzkopf, Will Smith, Sting, and Oprah Winfrey, to name a few.

JORDAN MCAULEY: What should someone know before requesting celebrity participation?

RITA TATEEL: Some of the questions you need to consider are: What exactly do you want the celebrity to do? Who do you want to appeal to by having the celebrity? Is it the media, the public, the attendees or sponsors? What do you want to accomplish by having a celebrity participate? Is it to add glitz and glamour, sell tickets, grab the public's attention, separate your campaign from the pack, or add credibility to the project? What are the demographics of your audience and attendees? What is your budget? What is the maximum that you are willing to spend for the right celebrity? Are you prepared to cover first-class expenses for the celebrity and at least one guest? Do you have access to any perks or gifts that will motivate a celebrity to say "yes"? These are some of the questions to which you should know the answers.

JM: If someone already knows how to contact celebrities using a service like ContactAnyCelebrity.com, why hire a company like the Celebrity Source?

RT: We are professionals in a very specialized field. Celebrity procurement and coordination is the total focus of our job on a day-to-day basis. We have developed many relationships within the celebrity community. In an industry where this is so important, our relationships enable us to get quicker and more positive responses. Large corporations, public relations firms, and ad agencies hire us even when they know how to access the celebrities themselves because they know that in the end, it's more cost- and time-effective to use our services.

JM: Does someone have to tell you whom they want, or do you suggest names?

RT: We start by asking you, our client, for a short wish list of names. This helps us understand what kind of star you are looking for. It also helps us make sure that there are realistic expectations. We then research additional names and make recommendations based on your objectives, budget and need.

JM: How are you able to determine which celebrity is right for a project?

RT: We maintain a data base of information on each celebrity that includes special interests, hobbies, hometown, favorite causes, sports skills, unique talents, and whether or not they have children or pets, among other things.

Often we get this information directly from the celebrities themselves after they have filled out our questionnaire. All of this information helps us make the right matches for our clients—matches that are meaningful, relevant and credible.

JM: Can you guarantee that you will find the right celebrity for a project?

RT: When you are dealing with celebrities, who are human beings like the rest of us, life happens. There are no guarantees; however we do not accept an account unless we feel that we can be successful for the client. Because of this, we have a 95 percent success rate.

JM: How much does it usually cost to hire a celebrity?

RT: Facts that affect how much a celebrity is paid depend on the celebrity, the level of his or her popularity, and the nature of the request. Generally speaking, a celebrity is paid a higher fee for endorsement deals and commercial requests than for most appearances or publicity campaigns.

Our fee (separate from the celebrity fee) is determined by the number of celebrities requested, whether there is a cause or charity involved, how complicated the coordination logistics are, and generally how much time we believe the request will take to fulfill.

JM: Are celebrities always paid?

RT: Celebrities are usually not paid for most nonprofit requests. However, perks and/or gifts are often a motivating factor to entice celebrity participation. An honorarium (which is usually lower than their standard fee) is often in order when a celebrity is asked to perform or participate in an activity that requires a great deal of preparation or rehearsal.

JM: When does your company get paid?

RT: Before we begin our work, we require a deposit that could range from 25 to 50 percent of our total fee, depending on the project. The balance of the fee is paid when the celebrity is confirmed, or upon a mutually agreeable timetable.

JM: Which aspects of celebrity procurement and coordination do you handle?

RT: We are a full-service celebrity company that handles all details concerning a celebrity's participation, including but not limited to: researching and developing a realistic list of potential celebrities who will stay within budget and meet our client's objectives; contacting and confirming the celebrity; and negotiating and acting as the liaison for contract fulfillment.

After a celebrity is confirmed, we coordinate the myriad of details and logistics necessary in order to have everything run smoothly. This may include coordinating ground transportation, travel, and accommodations; setting up briefing sessions when required; and acting as the liaison for content, script, or photo approval.

JM: How important are the perks and gifts that celebrities receive?

RT: Everyone enjoys receiving gifts, even celebrities. Sometimes perks, gifts and/or products can provide an extra incentive for the celebrities to say "yes" to a request. We often recommend that our clients build these items into a request or offer.

JM: What are some of the "dos and don'ts" of working with celebrities?

RT: 1) DON'T surprise celebrities with things you want them to do that were not part of the original request or contract. DO state everything you need from the celebrity up front and make sure that they are well-briefed as to what to expect and the purpose of their involvement.

2) DON'T ask celebrities to arrive too early, when there's no one around to show enthusiasm for their arrival.

3. DO set limits on the expenses that you are covering and let the celebrity know these limits in advance. DON'T state that all expenses are covered unless you are prepared to cover any amount.

4. DO provide a limousine if your budget allows. The easier you make it for a celebrity to attend, the more likely they will say "yes."

5. DON'T make any promises that you can't keep and DO keep all of the promises you make.

Hiring Celebrity Speakers

Have you ever wanted a celebrity to speak at an event other than a party, say for a seminar or corporate function? Hiring a celebrity to speak and maybe pose for photos with your attendees is a great way to increase ticket sales and create a memorable event.

So how much do celebrity speakers charge? As of this writing, big-name celebrities like Malcolm Gladwell of *The Tipping Point* and *Blink* charge $45,000. Political figures like Bill Clinton and Rudy Giuliani charge upward of $100,000. Jon Stewart charges $250,000 and Lance Armstrong charges $275,000.

But there are many celebrities whose speaking fees are much less. Contact various speaker bureaus for a list of their current clients and how much they charge. Most speakers are signed up with several bureaus, so be sure to shop for the best price. If you want to hire an author who isn't listed with a speaker bureau, contact the book's publishing company and ask for the publicity department to find out how to contact the author.

To learn more about hiring a celebrity for your event, check out my resource, *How to Hire a Celebrity for Your Event.... WITHOUT Getting Ripped Off!* (www.HowToHireACelebrity.com).

CHAPTER 10

Using Celebrity Voices

"Getting started using celebrity voice impression is easier that you think."

Susan Berkley
Unlock the Hidden Power of Your Voice
The Great Voice Company
www.GreatVoice.com

It's no surprise that large companies often hire celebrities to do voiceovers for radio and television commercials. Listeners respond better to voices they recognize, especially if from a likable personality. Celebrity voices are a great tool you can use to announce products, store or restaurant openings, charity fund-raisers, etc.

Voice blasting is a pretty new technology, so your customers won't be too aware of this Celebrity Leverage tactic. There are a number of voice-blast providers available, such as VoiceShot (www.VoiceShot.com). Simply sign up for the service online, upload your list of phone numbers, and record your message. The system then calls all your numbers, playing your message when someone answers or when an answering machine picks up the call.

As with e-mail blasts, you should only upload phone numbers for people with whom you have an existing business relationship. This means that the customer has previously purchased something from you, given you his phone number because he wants to be contacted, requested a free sample, etc.

You can either hire a celebrity to record your message or hire a celebrity impersonator. The neat thing about your celebrity-voiced message is that it will probably be heard by more than one person: The recipient saves it, then plays it for friends, family, coworkers, etc.

Once when I was younger, my dad came home from work excited because he had received a voicemail message from Kirk Cameron, who was starring on the hit TV show *Growing Pains* at the time. It was really him asking my dad to contribute money to a charity that had hired him to record the message. Of course my dad saved it, and when he got home, he played it for me, my brother, my sister, and my mom. I'm sure he also played it for friends and people at his office.

While your voice may be wonderful, most people aren't going to play your voice-blast message for others—no offense! But if you use a celebrity voice, they probably will. Imagine the possibilities for a new product, sale, store opening, club event, etc., and how many people might hear about it for each message sent.

Here's the good news: You don't have to pay big bucks to hire a real celebrity to record your messages (although you can do that if you want). For much less money, you can hire a celebrity voice impersonator, and your listener will never know the difference.

Insider Expert: Susan Berkley, The Great Voice Company

Susan Berkley is one of the most-listened-to voices in America as the "Voice of AT&T." She's a top professional voiceover artist and voiceover coach to talent all over the world as the founder and president of The Great Voice Company (www.GreatVoice.com). She's also the author of *Speak to Influence: How to Unlock the Hidden Power of Your Voice.*

"Getting started using celebrity voice impression is easier that you think," Susan says. She recommends using skilled celebrity voice impersonators and breaks down the process into three basic steps:

Step 1: Write your script. Keep it brief, about 75 words (30 seconds) or less. "If it's longer than that, your fake celebrity might annoy the listener," she warns. "Also, your voice talent won't be able to give you a quote without seeing your script."

Step 2: Choose your celebrity. "Make sure you choose a beloved A-list celebrity whose voice is well-known," Susan recommends. "People will definitely recognize an Arnold Schwarzenegger impression, but if you choose Brad Pitt or Angelina Jolie, they might be puzzled because the face is more distinct than the voice." And don't overlook dead celebrities, such as Marilyn Monroe and Elvis Presley.

Step 3: Find your talent. A Google search on "celebrity voice impressions" turned up a whopping 136,000 listings. "You can hear sample impressions on voice-talent Web sites," Susan points out. "Contact a talent you like." Prices vary but are typically in the $100 to $300 range for each voice impression.

"Delivery is easy," Susan notes. "The script is mailed to the talent with your turnaround time; they'll record it, and then you'll either receive an MP3 by e-mail or the message will be called into your phone system. Most talent you find on the Internet accept payment by credit card or PayPal."

One more thing. "Woody Allen is said to have once sued a sound-alike," Susan cautions. "Don't be surprised if your voice talent asks you to sign an indemnification agreement stating that the sound-alike impressions are for parody and satire purposes only and that you agree to hold them harmless from any damages associated with subsequent use."

THE NONDISCLOSURE CONCEPT

One school of thought on celebrity voiceovers believes it's better if the voice not say which celebrity is speaking. You've probably noticed television commercials where you recognized the voice, but the celebrity never said who he or she was. One example that comes to mind is Wendie Malick, who played Nina Van Horn on the television series *Just Shoot Me*. Malick's voice is recognizable, and she has recorded radio and television voiceovers for Marshall's. But the commercials never say who she is or make any type of reference to her.

According to the *Journal of Consumer Research* (JCR.WISC.edu), "television commercials featuring celebrity voiceovers are most influential when consumers can't identify which actor it belongs to." Research from the *Innovations Report* (www.Innovations-Report.com) supports this theory. "Different criteria should be used when selecting a celebrity for a voiceover than when selecting a celebrity to provide an endorsement. Voiceovers are most influenced simply by how much the celebrity is liked in the abstract. This general positive reaction to the celebrity influences brand evaluation even when the consumer has no idea the voiceover comes from the celebrity."

Growing up, my friend's mom was the voice of my hometown's Atlanta Hartsfield-Jackson International Airport (www.Atlanta-Airport.com). It was always fun to hear her say "welcome to Atlanta" whenever I returned from a trip. In the past, airports would use generic voices. Now, many airports are starting to use celebrity voices.

In Nashville, country singer Lee Ann Womach says: "This is Lee Ann Womack inviting you to relax and unwind in one of the airport's many restaurants. Thank you for choosing Nashville International

Airport." Wynonna Judd, Charlie Daniels, and members of Sugarland and Lonestar have also recorded announcements for the airport. According to a recent *USA Today* article, the goal is to "make [the announcements] stand out against the general sameness of air travel and to improve communication with travelers."

Nashville Airport was one of the first to switch from generic voices to celebrity voices. But Las Vegas Airport has used them since the 1970s, with stars such as Dick Clark, Phyllis Diller, Rich Little, Rodney Dangerfield and Bill Cosby recording the announcements – many times for free in exchange for the exposure.

When I was staying once at Nashville's Gaylord Opryland Report, here's what the little card by my phone said:

"Choose a special wake-up call from your favorite artist! You're in Nashville, known around the world as "Music City," so we've arranged for a few of our "music friends" to wake you up! Choose from Grand Ole Opry members like Trace Adkins, Vince Gill and Pam Tillis, or other popular artists like Kellie Pickler, Montgomery Gentry and Wynonna Judd. For a list of this week's celebrities, tune in to Channel 16 [on your TV]."

How many times have you returned home from a trip and told people about the wake-up calls at the hotel you stayed in? Unless the service forgot to wake you up and you missed something important, probably never. But imagine all the people who stay at the Gaylord Opryland Resort, then go home and tell their friends, family, and coworkers about getting woken up by their favorite country star?

Use celebrities in your business to add interest, excitement and customer satisfaction. Remember, you don't even have to hire real celebrities to record your messages—you can hire celebrity impersonators instead.

PART II:

Making
Yourself
Famous

Introduction by Paul Hartunian

"Celebrities are like cannon fodder for the media. Put a celebrity in a headline and the newspaper is almost guaranteed to sell more copies. It doesn't matter who the celebrity is or what they're doing. That means reporters would love an excuse to write about them—all you have to do is give it to them. Anyone can bring a celebrity into their story."

Paul Hartunian
Million Dollar Publicity Letter
Hartunian.com

Over the past few years, I've stressed a few important points over and over again. One has to do with the value of celebrity status and how publicity can easily and quickly help you get it.

You cannot overestimate the value of celebrity status that publicity gives you. One of the greatest benefits of publicity is that you don't have to do anything special to gain that celebrity status. To the vast majority of people, just the fact that you're on radio or TV or in newspapers and magazines makes you a celebrity.

You don't have to be a movie star or talk show host. You simply have to be interviewed by the media. Now am I saying that you'll have the same celebrity status as the current Oscar winners? Probably not. But in your own field, you may quickly become "the" go-to celebrity. And isn't that what you really want?

When I speak at seminars and show clips of me on *Johnny Carson*, *Phil Donahue*, *Jenny Jones*, *To Tell the Truth*, and other shows, I instantly become a celebrity. Without a doubt, I am the celebrity expert—and I have little competition.

It makes no difference whether you're an exterminator, a mortgage broker, a bakery owner, a roofer, or whatever, the media can make you a celebrity. People love to be around celebrities, regardless of their field. If you use publicity to gain celebrity status, you can have people feel the same way about you and your business.

Never, never, never underestimate the value of celebrity status to your business. And never, never, never underestimate the ability of the media to bestow that status on you.

Paul Hartunian (www.Hartunian.com) is often called "the man who sold the Brooklyn Bridge"—because he really did! Visit his Web site for tools and resources you can use to get free publicity for your business.

CHAPTER 11:

Becoming a Celebrity Expert in the Media

"Nothing happens until the cameras are rolling in America."
Mark Victor Hansen
Chicken Soup for the Soul

At the end of the day, most of your media opportunities will come down to your relationships with the media. Make sure you always send a real thank-you note (not just e-mail) to any reporter or journalist who interviews you or writes about you—no matter how small the write-up is.

Here's a true story: I once got mentioned in a national magazine, but it was a pretty small mention. I sent the reporter a thank-you note anyway, and about six months later he called. He told me he had risen to managing editor and was working on a story. "I've had your thank-you note sitting on my desk, so I immediately thought of you," he said. The story ran as an eight-page spread with photos, and the magazine even paid me for helping with the article. All because I sent a thank-you note that reminded the reporter who I was when he needed an expert on my topic.

Insider Interview: John Kremer, Open Horizons

John Kremer (www.BookMarket.com), one of the best-known book marketing experts and the author of *1001 Ways to Market Your Books*, agrees with me about the importance of developing relationships with the media:

All of marketing ultimately comes down to one thing: creating relationships. If you don't understand this basic principle, you will ultimately fail as a marketer. Indeed, you could fail in life as well.

Think about it: What is publicity? It is simply creating relationships with people in the media who, if they like your product, idea, or service, will pass that information on to their audience in the form of reviews, interviews or stories.

Think about it: What is distribution? It is simply creating relationships with retailers, wholesalers and sales representatives who will make your product available to retail customers

Think about it: What is product creation? It is simply creating relationships with technicians, suppliers, branding experts, and other people who can help you develop, design, produce, and complete a product, service or idea.

Wherever you look in business, relationships are what make things happen: networking, the old boys' network, the new girls' network, customer lists, sales reps visiting their customers, publicists talking with the media, luncheon meetings, trade shows, chat groups, newsletters, blogs and more. They all have one thing in common: Their primary purpose is to enhance communication and further relationships.

To help you create better relationships (especially with the people who count) and to assist you in marketing your products more effectively, here are a few basic principles you should follow:

1. Create your "Kremer 100" list. OK, I named this after myself because it needed a branded name.

Don't try to be friends with thousands or millions of people. You can't do it. Focus on 100 key media and marketing contacts (if you don't have time to focus on 100, make your list 25 or 50 people). Develop this Kremer 100 list into a data base with their addresses, phone numbers, fax numbers, e-mail addresses and URLS. Also include their cell phone numbers and perhaps even their home phone numbers.

Your goal is to get to know their likes and dislikes, what moves them, and what they look for in a good story (if they are media) or a good product (if they are buyers). You also want to get to know how they like to get information. Do they prefer e-mail, fax, phone or mail?

2. Be persistent. After you've developed a data base of key contacts, you must get in touch with them on a regular basis–at least once a month. Tell them something new with each contact. If you ever get an opportunity to meet them in person, jump at the chance. But the key is continual follow-up. It makes all the difference in whether or not you establish a real relationship.

3. Create a word-of-mouth army. Because 80 percent of all books are sold by word-of-mouth (book marketing is my area of specialty), your primary goal in marketing is to create a core group of people who will spark that word-of-mouth. Think of these people as the officers for your word-of-mouth army, because what you ultimately want to create is an army of people talking about your book, idea, product, service or whatever. In that army, you'll have privates, corporals, sergeants, lieutenants, majors, colonels and generals.

The moment someone meets you, they've self-promoted themselves to at least a corporal. If they ask a question or make another move to talk more with you, count them a sergeant. If they buy something from you, promote them to lieutenant. You get the idea. In my *1001 Ways to Market Your Books* army, I have at least two five-star generals: Jack Canfield (www.JackCanfield.com) and Mark Victor Hansen (www.MarkVictorHansen.com). They've earned every star. (If you don't like the analogy of an army, then think of it as participants in a parade, fan club or party).

4. Become a people person. At home in Taos, New Mexico, I'm a quiet, shy fellow. Here, few people know who I am or what I do. But when I go out to speak or to attend trade shows, I become a new person—a people person. Fortunately, I enjoy that interaction with the public. If you're going to become a successful relationship builder, you too will have to cultivate that fun feeling when you go out into the public. If you genuinely care about people, you'll have no problem facing them. Just open your heart and let your caring come out.

When speaking to the Women Writers of the West conference several years ago, I realized that when I talked about creating relationships, I was really talking about making friends. Because that is what every good marketer really does: They make friends. When you begin to think of marketing in this way, everything about marketing becomes more fun. Suddenly, there is no foreignness, no fear, no feeling of inadequacy. We can all make friends. It's a talent we've had since we were children. Use it.

You may not be a household name–yet–but there are strategies you can follow to become famous. What you *really* want is to be famous in your area of expertise — your "niche."

For example, if you're a real-estate agent, you want people to think of you whenever they think of real estate. You may not be known all over the world, like Donald Trump, but you can easily become the "go-to" agent for your local area. You can do the same thing if you're a doctor, lawyer, mortgage broker, plumber, fitness trainer, plastic surgeon, massage therapist, etc. It doesn't matter what your area of expertise is–you can become a celebrity expert.

Recently I attended Bill and Steve Harrison's Publicity Summit (www.PublicitySummit.com) in New York City. For several days, television and radio producers, magazine editors, freelance writers and journalists met with authors and heard their one-minute pitch—sort of like speed dating for experts.

I met an editor from *Star* magazine who I thought might be interested in writing about my *Celebrity Black Book* (www.CelebrityBlackBook.com). However, she told me that she was really only looking for medical experts such as plastic surgeons, psychologists, dermatologists and others who could comment on celebrity stories in her magazine. ("Has so and so had a facelift? Doctor X says yes!")

Most of these celebrity magazines are looking for experts to comment on what the stars are doing. The media quotes and interviews experts all the time. Being quoted in major magazines adds to your "expert" credibility and helps turn you into a celebrity. So if you want to really become a celebrity expert, the first step is to write a book. The second step is to appear in major media.

Insider Interview: Dan Janal, PR Leads

Dan Janal is founder and president of PR Leads (www.MyPRLeads.com), a service that connects experts with the media. He is a frequent speaker on the topics of publicity, marketing and the Internet and is author of *Dan Janal's Guide to Marketing on the Internet*. *USA Today* called Dan a "true Internet pioneer" because he was on the PR team that launched America Online. He also directed the PR launch of *Grolier's Electronic Encyclopedia*, the first consumer software program ever produced on CD-ROM.

JORDAN MCAULEY: Why is it so important to become a celebrity in your field?

DAN JANAL: Experts get respect. Experts get hired. Experts get their books and their products sold. It's as simple as that. When you become an expert, you become a celebrity in your field. You're an authority. People bow down. We look at a movie and we don't know anything about it except that it was directed by one of today's famous directors. Well, it stands a good chance of being a good movie. Or there's a famous actor in the movie like Dustin Hoffman or Meryl Streep. Odds are, it's a pretty good movie. You may take a chance on it knowing little else except the reputation of the expert—or the celebrity, in this case.

One of my clients for PR Leads (www.MyPRLeads.com) is a motivational speaker named Patrick Snow. He wrote a book called *Creating Your Own Destiny: How to Get Exactly What You Want Out of Life*. After we were able to get his picture on the front page of *USA Today*, he went from being a $2,500 speaker to a $5,000 speaker. He was able to double his rate overnight—but that wasn't the biggest news. The biggest news was that before, when he was a $2,500 speaker, everyone tried to negotiate his fees lower. But after he was on the front page of *USA Today*, meeting planners just accepted his fee. That's the power of publicity and that's why you want to be perceived as an expert in your local market or in your field

JM: How does someone begin to become a celebrity expert in his or her field?

DJ: One of my friends in the National Speakers Association (www.NSASpeaker.org) is Tom Winninger. He has dominated three niches; one of them is the power tools industry. When someone in the steel or hardware industry need to hire a keynote speaker, they go to Tom because everyone knows him. He's written articles in their journals, done volunteer work for their associations, and really networked and marketed himself within his field. That's why no one else can penetrate it—because he owns it. He dominates his niche. There are thousands of niches like that that you can dominate

Dan Kennedy (www.DanKennedyPresents.com) always refers back to one of his clients who dominates the pug dog industry. One of my clients is an expert in parrot training and parrot diseases. How many people own parrots? Millions! You could spend your whole life just dealing with parrots and not have to worry about any other kind of bird under the sun. Think of being the niche dominator instead of the jack of all trades. That is the first step to becoming a celebrity expert.

Generalists do not make as much money as specialists. Think about doctors. If you are a general doctor, you get good business. You may have a nice family practice, but if you were a specialist in heart attacks, or gallbladders, or whatever, you would make a lot more money. The same is true with other fields. You could be a marketing expert but if you are everything to everyone, you're not going to be able to charge as much as if you were the marketing go-to person in the pharmaceuticals industry.

Pricing is also important. Just by charging higher prices, you'll be perceived as an expert. In fact, if your prices are not high enough, people will assume you're not an expert and will just take anyone who walks in the door. This is one of the ironies of life. No one wants to spend $400 an hour for an attorney, but would you spend $75 an hour for an attorney? Not for a good one.

JM: Is it better to become famous in more than one niche or to focus on just one?

DJ: My business coach is Mark LeBlanc (www.MarkLeBlanc.com). He says that if you own just 7 percent of your market, you will have more work than you can ever handle. In other words, if there are 4,000 people in the National Speakers Association and 7 percent of them are my clients, that is a lot of people. If each of them wanted to consult with me for an hour a month, there are not enough hours in a month. It's as simple as that. I think you should start with dominating one niche. Think about how hard you want to work. Also, think about how you can rework your material for other niches.

JM: What are some of the best ways to leverage the publicity someone receives?

DJ: One of the great fallacies of publicity is that people actually read newspapers and magazines and act on what they see. That is not why we get publicity. No one reads every word of every page of every newspaper they subscribe to, so the chances of them seeing that wonderful article about you on page 16 of the *Wall Street Journal* are pretty small—but it is a great marketing tool. Publicity is not an end unto itself. It is the means to an end and the way for you to create incredible marketing materials so that you can go out to the world and say, "I have been quoted in the *Wall Street Journal*" or "the *New York Times* wrote about me." This kind of branding really does help.

Here are a couple of quick things you can do. First, when you are quoted in a major newspaper, immediately send out an e-mail to everyone on your list with a subject that says, "Dan is quoted in *USA Today*." In the message, say, "Read Dan's comments about new trends in online publicity at www.usatoday.com/whatever." Some people will click through and read about you, and that is great. Other people are too busy and won't read it, but that's OK because they'll still say, "Wow! Dan was quoted in *USA Today*." This gives you another chance to stay in touch with your clients, prospective clients, and mother-in-law so she finally knows what you are doing for a living.

If you print it out, you can frame it and put it up in your office or place of business. Use a yellow highlighter to highlight your name and the quote. If you are a dry cleaner, then suddenly you become the celebrity dry cleaner because you were quoted in the newspaper. If you're a doctor, you have it in your waiting room framed with a dozen other articles. Your patients are not going to seek a second opinion from anyone else and will follow your advice because they figure you are the celebrity expert. You are the one they need to listen to.

It's important to have a press section on your Web site, but don't just leave your press in the press section. Use your front page to say, "Dan has been quoted in 53 newspapers including the *New York Times*, *Wall Street Journal*, and *Investor's Business Daily*." Take screenshots of any TV shows you've been on and put them on your Web site. A picture tells a thousand words, and having visuals of you on TV shows adds instant credibility. Don't make them hunt. Let them know that you are the expert.

JM: What's the difference between being a "celebrity" and being a "celebrity expert?"

DJ: There's an interesting differentiation. When people tell me they want to be the next Oprah, I tell them point blank that it isn't going to happen. I use this example: You are the keynote speaker at a conference. Everyone at that conference is bowing down to you and asking for your opinion, saying "sign my book" and wanting a photo and all those wonderful things that happen when you do the right things to market yourself. But once you get to the airport, no one knows you at all. You could be sitting in first class next to the president of the bar association or someone else important in his own field. You think he's nobody, he thinks you're nobody. That's the difference. People outside of your niche don't know you.

Because we only have so much time and energy and money, it's really important to dominate your niche and let the rest of the world go by. I had dinner recently with a famous author and contributor to *The Secret*. He is way up there but wanted to know how he could become even more famous so that everyone in America knew him. I said, "If everyone in America knows about you, how would that change your life? Could you serve them all?" He said probably not, because he can only serve a certain group of people who are interested in his area of expertise. I told him to just focus on that one group, because he does not have enough time, energy or money to educate the entire world about who he is. It really pays to be focused.

JM: What level of fame can you really hope to achieve as a celebrity expert?

DJ: I think people can hope to dominate their industry. You can go from nowhere to dominating your field within a couple of years. In fact, I recently listened to a great tape by Brian Tracy (www.BrianTracy.com). He said that everyone who is an expert in their field today started out not knowing anything in that field. It is so true. Everyone had to study and read and learn and have life experiences to get to a certain point. Brian makes the point that if you read a couple of books about your industry every year, at the end of five years you will have more knowledge than most people in your industry because no one reads anymore. In a very short time, you really could become better than 99 percent of the people in your industry, and then you dominate it. You are the go-to guy. I think that is very doable.

Pick a niche you have fun with and enjoy. Do not do parrots if you don't like parrots. Otherwise it is going to be a very boring, difficult journey. Become an expert in a field that you love. That way you'll have fun along the way to becoming a celebrity expert, and fun is what work and life should be about.

Insider Interview: Robyn Spizman, Author

One of the country's foremost gift and product experts, Robyn Spizman (www.RobynSpizman.com) has appeared on local and national media—her weekly radio show on Star 94 FM in Atlanta with Cindy & Ray; multiple appearances on CNN; national talk shows such as *The Today Show*. She has also been covered extensively in national magazines and newspapers across America. Spizman's books include *Make It Memorable*, *The Giftionary*, *Where's Your Wow?*, and the *Author 101* series (with Rick Frishman).

JORDAN MCAULEY: What would you say to someone who wants to become a celebrity expert?

ROBYN SPIZMAN: Unless you're already a celebrity with a recognizable platform, the key is to build a platform by starting locally in your hometown. My first appearance was thanks to a craft book I had just written. I started appearing on the local NBC affiliate when I first got started in 1981 and became a how-to expert on Atlanta's leading talk show called Noonday.

As I wrote and coauthored many books on other topics like parenting, entertaining kids and gift-giving, I built a credible name as a parenting expert and a super shopper. As time went on, I was interviewed by many national newspapers and magazines. I studied the marketplace and recognized that there were no shopping experts at the time, which was well before home shopping shows, especially in Atlanta. It's important to become an authority in your own backyard first, because that's a great way to build your expertise and skills.

You must ask yourself, "What am I doing that's original?" Teaming up with smart people in the know is also very important. I've never done anything that's not a reflection of my sincere interest.

JM: How did you get your own radio show on Star 94 in Atlanta?

RS: After writing the book The Giftionary, I felt I was ready to branch out and propose a radio show. I worked on all the show ideas for a year and how I would do it. It's important to understand the medium you're going into, but it's equally important to do something unique in the marketplace. I pitched the idea to Start 94's general manager, and it was a match made in heaven. I now have a daily online site at www.Star94.com and a monthly show called The Giftionary, which is so much fun and a very informative gift-giving show.

Every media outlet is unique and requires extreme preparation. Keeping track of all your appearances, print articles and publicity is essential. I've kept a stack from 26 years of being mentioned in the media, from USA Today to the New York Times to most of the major magazines. I have a track record that's substantiated, and I have a reel from my television appearances prepared whenever that's requested. They key is to be prepared and ready for success. Still, the bigger picture is to make sure you're doing something of value that serves a media outlet. It's all about providing something meaningful to their listeners, readers or viewers.

JM: What are some tips for making your media appearances memorable?

RS: Do really great work and be the best you can be at what you do. That sounds so cliché, but it's true. Always raise the bar. The key is you want to be phenomenal. You have to work on your craft, your style, your wardrobe, and your ability to be remarkable. Ask yourself, "What kind of impression did I make in one minute?" Be thoughtful. Are you considerate of the media? Do you over-deliver? Do you do more work than you're supposed to? These are the questions you have to ask yourself.

The foundation of everything, I believe, is to be grateful for the opportunities I receive and to work ten times harder than the next person. If I'm going to make it memorable, I want to leave them wanting me back and make them look good. It's not about me; it's about the integrity of what I do and simply knowing that I did the best job possible. Did you make the viewer or listener smarter? Did you make them smile? Did you give them something of value with a takeaway? Make sure you're providing meaning and helping the viewer.

Are you listening to and watching the shows you want to be on? For example, people call me up and say, "I want to be on your segment." Sometimes they don't even know what I do. I don't put people on, I put products on. So the key is to know the show.

JM: Any tips for hiring a PR firm?

RS: I have never taken for granted the fact that someone knows who I am. My husband runs a full-service book, author, and expert public relations firm called The Spizman Agency (www.SpizmanAgency.com). I'm one of their clients, and I take media relations very seriously. To me, it's really all about building relationships with the media.

Use professionals because you can't do everything yourself. Have a better understanding of publicity. Read expert's books and invest in their help. A great PR person can be one of your greatest assets. But they are only as good as their client. You have to have the goods, and often the timing has to be right for your message. Most people try PR and then, when it doesn't work in the first three or even six months, give up. I'm here to tell you that I've been in the public eye for more than 26 years, and a solid public relations campaign with repeated media appearances does work, will gain momentum, and ultimately will provide benefit for your message.

CHAPTER 12:

Becoming a Celebrity Author

"Some years ago I wrote a book entitled *How to Sell Your Services*. Just before the manuscript went to the publisher, it occurred to me to request some of the well-known men of the United States to write letters of endorsement to be published in the book."

Napoleon Hill
The Law of Success

The idea of writing a book can be intimidating. If you're uncomfortable expressing yourself on paper or are burdened with your day-to-day work, it can be downright overwhelming. However, becoming a published author is one of the best ways to become a celebrity, especially in your field.

Writing a book should be a crucial part of your professional goals. Regardless of the type of business you're running, having a book distinguishes you and sets you apart from the competition. It instantly transforms you from Joe Smith, owner of XYZ, into Joe Smith, bestselling author of *How to XYZ in Ten Easy Steps*.

Just as celebrities can make your product or company more visible, so can writing a book. It enhances your status and turns you into a celebrity in your field as soon as it's published—or a big celebrity if your book sells well. Note that I'm talking about nonfiction books. Fiction books can turn you into a celebrity author, but it's much more difficult than with nonfiction written about you and your area of expertise. Nonfiction also can promote you or your business, as you'll see below.

The Benefits of Being a Published Author

Writing a book helps you:

- Get publicity in print and national media.
- Appear on local and national TV and radio programs.
- Speak at local, regional and national meetings or seminars.
- If you already speak, get paid higher fees.
- Expand your client or customer base by establishing your credibility as an expert.
- Generate leads by including "bounceback" offers in your book.

It's important to point out that unless you happen to get a large book advance from a major publisher, you're probably not going to get rich from book sales. The money comes from the credibility and expert status you achieve from having the book, plus ancillary information products you can create from the book, such as courses, consulting, speaking engagements and workshops. For more about creating information products from your book, visit the Information Marketing Association at www.Info-Marketing.org.

You should view your book as a way to get more customers—sort of like an expanded business card. Imagine when people ask you for your business card, you hand them your book instead. They're going to remember you, and they will be less likely to throw away or lose your book than they would a business card.

Creating Your Platform

There's one word that's become a sort of buzzword among publishers—"platform." Whenever you talk to an editor, publicist or literary agent, this word will inevitably come up. "What's your platform?" is a polite way that publishers ask how the author will put forth extra time and energy to help sell books.

If you're a first-time author, this question can be confusing. All it really boils down to is showing a publisher that even though you're not yet a household name, you already have a following—and not only will these people be interested in buying your book when it comes out, you'll also help the publisher reach these prospective buyers. There's no one ideal platform, but you'll need some, if not all, of the following:

E-mail List

This can be a list of your clients, people who have attended your workshops or events, visitors to your Web site, etc. If you have a news-letter (paid or unpaid), this is your subscriber list. If you don't have a list, consider a joint venture with someone who does. Authors do that more often than you might realize. In fact, you've probably received e-mails from an author promoting another author's book.

Generally, the larger your e-mail list the better. However, a targeted list of people interested in you and your company is preferable to a sizable, generic list of people who might not care about the subject of your book. If you're not yet collecting e-mails from people who visit your Web site, that's the first and best place to start.

Consider giving away a free report or e-book (perhaps the book you're writing or a chapter from the book as a downloadable PDF file) in exchange for the person's name and e-mail address. Also, collect e-mail addresses at all your appearances, trade shows and book signings by having people give you their business cards or fill out a form. So you're not accused of spamming, be sure to let them know you want to add them to your e-mail list.

To collect e-mail addresses and send messages to your list, I recommend online service GetResponse (www.MyGetResponse.com).

Having an up-to-date, easy-to-use data base of all your customers, clients, and new daily leads will help you enormously when your book is published. You'll be able to quickly send out an email blast letting your contacts know that your book is available as soon as it comes out.

Newspaper Column, Radio Show, or Blog

If you're already writing or speaking about a topic, a publisher will view your book proposal more favorably than someone who doesn't have these outlets. Editors don't expect you to write for the New Yorker, but you need to show that you're building an audience. Writing a column for a local magazine or newspaper is a good first start. From there, you can build up to trade magazines in your industry. Appearing on a local radio station as a frequent guest is another strategy. Having a widely read blog is also a great way to build a platform.

Speaking Engagements

Large publishers will often ask for your speaking engagement calendar for the past year and the next six months as a way to evaluate your platform and the potential to sell books at these speaking gigs. So if you're not already speaking regularly, you'll want to start.

Volunteer to talk to your local Chamber of Commerce breakfast or networking meeting. If your industry holds a regular convention, see if you can participate in a panel discussion. If you're afraid to get up in front of a group to speak, join your local Toastmasters (www.Toastmasters.org) organization. Toastmasters meetings allow you to start small and practice in a safe environment. The more you practice speaking, the more your anxiety will disappear.

Why is your "platform" so important? Well, while you may assume that all books are available in large chain bookstores or other major retailers, that isn't the case. With so many books published each year, booksellers simply cannot stock every title. The publisher needs your "platform" to persuade booksellers that there will be a demand for your book. So the burden is on the author to help promote and sell the book as well as write it.

Insider Interview: Penny Sansevieri, Author Marketing Experts, Inc.

Penny Sansevieri (www.AMarketingExpert.com) is the best-selling author of *From Book to Bestseller: An Insider's Guide to Publicizing and Marketing Your Book*. She's also a marketing consultant who works with authors and has published books herself. I asked Penny for her advice on how authors can build a platform, and we also discussed why authors might consider the self-published route.

JORDAN MCAULEY: What's your take on why a "platform" is so important for authors?

PENNY SANSEVIERI: A platform isn't who you know, but who knows you. It's your sphere of influence, and to a publisher, it means a built-in audience who will possibly buy your book. Having a platform can be crucial to furthering your career. If your ultimate goal is to ink a deal with a major publisher, then a platform isn't just crucial—it's mandatory.

JM: Besides creating a Web site, what are some ways people can use the Internet to develop a platform?

PS: Network with bloggers in your market. These are folks who can read, review or endorse your book. Also, syndicating articles on the Internet is a great way to get the word out about your message and your book. Get onto social networking sites like Facebook (www.Facebook.com), Squidoo (www.Squidoo.com), and LinkedIn (www.LinkedIn.com). Then use the traffic that comes to that page and drive it to your Web site using free offers or specials. And don't forget to collect the names and e-mail addresses of people who get your free offer.

JM: What factors should someone consider before deciding whether to self-publish or choose a traditional publisher?

PS: First, I don't think there's anything wrong with self-publishing so long as your book doesn't look self-published. Save the arts and crafts for your kids and publish something that's letter-perfect and has a book cover that will attract, rather than repel, readers.

The key to remember is that because the barriers to entry in self-publishing are minimal, the market has been flooded with books. It's no longer an issue of whether you can publish, but whether potential readers will find your book. Having access on Amazon.com is great, but it can't replace worldwide or even national distribution.

Getting a distributor used to be easy, until the per-day number of books published hit 500, and now it's even higher. Consequently, these distribution channels have gotten severely clogged. While you may publish a quality book, there are thousands of other less-than-acceptable books ahead of yours.

So what can you do? Market, market, market, and make sure you're spending sufficient time pulling in your marketing support online.

JM: Any other thoughts on publishing you'd like to share?

PS: Consider this: Regardless of how you publish, you should always be engaged in your own success. Yes, publishing companies have marketing departments, and if you're lucky, they'll spend some personal time on your book. More than likely, though, the marketing person has many, many titles to take care of, and personalized attention isn't always possible. Expect to manage your own marketing and publicity. Even if you outsource it, you should still plan to do some of it yourself.

My final point is that publishers will often pick up an author or book that has been self-published in a previous life. Why? Because if they find a book that's doing well, they know two things. First, they know they've found an author who knows how to market their book, and secondly, they've found a book that already has an audience. Sometimes, if the publisher feels that the book has sold out of its marketing, they might offer to buy your next book.

The key to remember is that in a publishing world that's highly uncertain, when a publisher finds an author who has a platform and isn't afraid to use it, that alone can be the key to your success.

There are three main routes to print publication that I'll discuss in this section. Also, know that you can sell downloadable e-books from your Web site. But while e-books are a great way to test your book, they don't build credibility as well as a printed book does.

The three main publishing routes are: (1) self-publishing, (2) vanity publishing, and (3) traditional publishing. Under the umbrella of self-publishing, there's another form of publishing called "print on demand," which is a great option for first-time authors. Because of that, I'll address print-on-demand publishing first.

Thanks to advances in digital printing, you can now start small using a print-on-demand service such as Lulu, Amazon's CreateSpace, Blurb, or Lightning Source so you don't have to print 5,000 books before you know if it will sell. If you want to change your cover, title, or add some celebrity endorsements, you can do so at any time.

Some of the services above are also able to get your book listed on Amazon.com and other online retailers. They might also be able to list it with the two major book wholesalers, Baker & Taylor and Ingram. Being with these wholesalers makes your book available to all bookstores that want to order it.

Not that long ago, self-publishing was known as "vanity" publishing and wasn't well-regarded. Today, however, especially for nonfiction titles, many authors prefer to self-publish their books because it allows them more control over the entire process.

The self-publishing route means that you write the manuscript and then hire or outsource people to handle the editing, design, production and printing. With today's sophisticated design and graphics software, it's getting harder and harder to tell a self-published book from a book published by a traditional publishing house.

With a vanity publisher (also known as subsidy publishing), you pay the publisher to design the book and handle the printing. You'll need to determine how many copies to print. The quantity will depend on whether you're selling the book yourself or working with a distributor to make the book available online as well as in brick-and-mortar bookstores.

With a traditional publisher, you're generally paid in advance against royalties and are given a deadline by which you are required to turn in your manuscript. Depending on the size of the publisher and the scope of your project, you may have a developmental editor in addition to the editor who acquired your book, plus a marketing person and maybe a publicist. It's the publisher's responsibility to handle distribution of your book.

If you want to learn more about traditional publishing, including how to get a large advance from a major publisher, I recommend publishing expert Susan Harrow's *Get a Six-Figure Book Advance* (www.6FigureBookAdvance.com).

The reality is that publishing is a business, and like any other business, it's competitive. Millions of books are published each year, and many quickly disappear compared with the few titles that become best-sellers. You—the author—have to spend just as much time and effort, if not more, on the marketing and publicity of your book as you did on the writing, regardless of how it's being published. You can also outsource this work to a publicist.

This isn't meant to be discouraging. After all, when you were starting your business, you probably had naysayers cautioning you about the record number of companies that never lasted past five years. However, you were convinced that you had a sound business plan, and you forged ahead. If you have a concept for a book and you feel that it will help you expand your company, then you should start writing it.

Insider Interview: Anne McIndoo, So You Want to Write!

Ann McIndoo (www.SoYouWantToWrite.com), the author of *So You Want to Write a Book*, teaches people how to write a book in just three days. In this interview, Ann McIndoo shares some of her processes.

JORDAN MCAULEY: Tell us a little about your approach.

ANN MCINDOO: I like to compare writing to golfing. If you're a golfer, you set your tee time. You get your equipment. The whole week while you're planning for your golf game on Sunday, what are you doing? You get all excited, right? You're preparing. So when you get to the golf green on Sunday, you're so excited that it doesn't matter whether you have a crummy game or not. You had fun, yes? It's the same with writing. And when you're ready to write, you'll write amazing stuff.

Like with golf, you have to be prepared in three places when writing. You have to be prepared in your inner game—what's going on in your head. You have to be prepared in your body—are you ready to write? And you need to be prepared in your environment. So I came up with a little thing I call my "Writer's Power Tools."

JM: What are your "writer's power tools"?

AM: These are my writer's power scripts, what I say to myself; my power moves, how I get my body ready; and my power anchors, what I have around me to get ready to write. What I do with my power scripts is when I get ready to write, I say, "OK, I'm going to write." I make my writing appointments, I have my writing calendar, and I decide that my outcome is to have this book done ,and I have my deadline.

JM: How do you schedule your time?

AM: At the beginning of every week on Sunday night, I take out my writing calendar. And I say, "OK, on Monday, I'm going to write for 20 minutes. I don't have time to write on Tuesday. On Wednesday, I'm going to write for a half-hour. On Friday, I'm going to spend two hours." So I make my writing appointments. After I make my writing appointments, I keep my writing appointments. Because no writing appointments means no book. It's that easy.

JM: You also have writing rituals?

AM: Before I go to my writing appointment, I get ready. That's when I have my writing ritual. Let's say I set my writing appointment for 6 o'clock in the morning. I like to write early, when it's all quiet. So I'm in my pajamas, and I go over to my writing area with a cup of tea and my little dog. I put on some soft music with no words. I light my candle, and I have all my stuff around me. I have my cup with my pencils, and my post-up notes I'll use with my ideas. And I also have a couple of things I wear. I have my author hat. When I put this hat on, it means I'm serious. These anchors put me in that really great writing place—that I'm a writer, and this is what I'm going to do this morning.

I also have my writing script. I clap my hands and get them all warm, because I have this belief that I have all of these things inside of me that want to come out. So I clap my hands and say, "Yes, yes, yes, I can't wait to write! This is going to be so much fun. I can't believe that I'm so lucky I get to do this today." And after saying those words, I'm in the mood. I really want to write!

JM: What can someone expect using this writing process?

AM: You're going to write the most amazing stuff, the most brilliant stuff that's inside you waiting to get out. You know it's all in there. So it's about having your head, your body and your writing environment ready. And you don't have to have a big fancy place. Sometimes my favorite writing spot is a plastic lounge chair by the pool. I just have to know that that's where I'm going to do it. And I see myself; I visualize myself getting there ready to write.

JM: What else do you suggest?

AM: The next time you order business cards, or you can order a special batch of business cards, use the word "writer." At least while you're writing your book—then replace it with "author" when you finish. Because unless you put yourself in that place and find its identity, it's going to be really difficult to manifest, and it's not going to want to come out.

Also, think about your power script. What are you going to say to yourself as you get ready to write? Think of something you already do that's a lot of fun. What do you say to yourself then? Think about it, and write those words down. That's how you're going to come up with your writing script.

It's the same thing with your power move. What do you do to get ready? The more you practice doing it, the faster you'll be ready and prepared to write. If you've already been writing before, think of a time when you wrote something that was just amazing—and then replicate it. If you haven't written a lot, think of what would be a great way to write, and then go there.

I also created my writer's kit. Inside I have my pencil and my paper and my writer's calendar. I have my spiral notebook, my outline, and my storyboard in there. Get yourself someplace where you can have all your stuff, and you can be ready to write whenever you want to write.

JM: How would you sum up your writing process?

AM: Basically, there are two rules—first, keep your writing appointment. The second is, when you make your writing appointment, have a reasonable goal. Write down what you believe you're going to do. If you make a writing appointment for fifteen minutes, keep it.

OTHER WAYS TO WRITE YOUR BOOK

Hire a Ghostwriter

If you have some money to spare (ghostwriters usually are not cheap), you can hire someone else to write your book, even though you retain the title of author. Or you can hire a journalist or another writer to interview you for a couple of days, then turn the interview into a book. Some publishing companies, such as Advantage Media Group (www.AdvantageFamily.com), will do this for you.

Celebrities use ghostwriters all the time when they "write a book." Ever wondered how people who suddenly become famous can suddenly publish a book? They (or their publishing companies, since most celebrities are traditionally published) hire a journalist who sits down with them for a few days, interviewing them about important aspects of their lives they want to share. The journalist then puts the book together.

For example, Neil Strauss is a contributing editor at Rolling Stone who has interviewed such stars as Madonna and Dave Navarro for the magazine. He is also the author of his own best-selling book The Game but has ghostwritten books for Marilyn Manson, Motley Crue and Jenna Jameson.

Many freelance writers are available to ghostwrite books for businesspeople who don't know how, don't want to bother, or just don't have the time. Mahesh Grossman (www.AuthorsTeam.com) author of *Write a Book Without Lifting a Finger*, says 43 percent of all published authors use a ghostwriter to create the kind of books you see on the best-seller lists. He says anyone can have a book within 90 days of hiring a ghostwriter.

Be the Messenger Instead of the Message

This is what Jack Canfield and Mark Victor Hansen did with their hugely popular *Chicken Soup for the Soul* series. These books are merely collections of other people's stories, yet Mark Victor Hansen and Jack Canfield get the credit.

The book's contributors didn't get to appear on *Oprah*—Mark and Jack did. This was also the concept of *The Secret*. Rhonda Byrne simply compiled quotes and advice from experts, both living and dead, about using the Law of Attraction to get what you desire.

Joe Vitale, best-selling author of *The Attractor Factor* who was featured in *The Secret*, does this with other experts' articles. His recent books *The Key* and *The Seven Lost Secrets of Success* are mostly compilations of articles from other experts on the Law of Attraction. And again, he gets the credit for the book!

Recycle Your Existing Content

If you don't want to write (or don't want to start from scratch), you should recycle your content. Well-known authors such as Suze Orman and Martha Stewart do this often. For example, Martha will write an article for her magazine on carrot recipes. Then she'll take that article and make it a chapter in her new cookbook. Then she'll take that chapter and make it an episode on her television show. Get the point?

If you're used to writing articles, make a list of the chapters you want to include in your book, and then think of each chapter as an article. Breaking your book up into chunks this way keeps you from getting overwhelmed. You should also look at past articles you've written for your e-mail list or print newsletter, if you have one, and see if you can use those.

If you write a blog, do this with your blog posts as well. Some authors such as Seth Godin have created entire books from blogs. His recent book, *Small Is the New Big*, is merely a collection of his most popular blog posts. In fact, Lulu holds a contest each year called the "Lulu Blooker Prize" that features books created from blogs.

Having a blog is not only a great way to communicate with customers and boost your search engine rankings but is also a great way to organize content for your book. After you've been blogging for a while, you can even take your posts and turn them into a book as Seth Godin did.

I recommend TypePad for all your blogging needs. Many people like and recommend WordPress, but you have to install it and deal with technical issues yourself. TypePad is easy to use, and it hosts the software for you. All you have to do is post, and TypePad takes care of the rest.

Use Public Domain Material

I wouldn't suggest using public domain material for your entire book because you want to be perceived as the expert. However, public domain material can provide you with a starting point for your book or the majority of the information for some of your chapters

Public domain means the copyright for the work no longer exists, so anyone is free to use it. Joe Vitale did this with his book *There's a Customer Born Every Minute.* He used P.T. Barnum's biography, which was in the public domain, as the basis for this book on attracting customers by using publicity in fun and creative ways.

For more information on using public domain materials, I recommend Yanik Silver's Public Domain Goldmine.

Insider Interview: Robyn Spizman, Author

There's no denying that writing a book takes time, energy and commitment. Still, most authors would agree that identifying themselves as "author of XYZ" is invaluable.

In this interview, Robyn Spizman (www.RobynSpizman.com), author of the *Giftionary, Make It Memorable,* and many other books, talks about her experiences in the book world.

JORDAN MCAULEY: What can writing a book do for a business owner?

ROBYN SPIZMAN: A book helps you get more speaking opportunities, your business becomes more well-known, you attract more clients, and you make a difference in the world. It's also a valuable opportunity to share what you care about. It also makes you feel really good to help make people smarter and brighter.

JM: How has writing a book helped make you into a celebrity expert?

RS: I've been fortunate to be on the air in Atlanta for 26 years now. I began on the air because I had written my very first book. I kept showing up with creative ideas, and the producers kept inviting me back. I was always reinventing myself because the trends would change.

I always cared deeply about how I was helping the consumer. I was a mom with young children, so I thought of what was most important and on my radar. I was authentic, which I know made a difference.

It was a long, steady journey to becoming known. After I was on a local television network, my producer recommended me to CNN when they called looking for a consumer advocate to report on toys. That provided me with a wonderful vote of confidence. One opportunity leads to the next. What's my motto? "You're only as good as your last segment." My work ethic was just to keep showing up and doing a great job, because that could be my last segment. After a while, national talk shows started calling because they were aware of my books.

The book was a calling card. I did many interviews, no matter how big or small, with little radio stations and newspapers all over the country. Now I'm interviewed frequently, with newspaper and radio shows calling me.

JM: What are some tips for holding a memorable book release party?

RS: Great, memorable parties are about the guests. They make the guests feel at home, taken care of, involved and entertained. You want your book cover visible somewhere, and for them to go home with your book. The key is to match the theme of your book. Think of fun ways to involve your guests so they'll remember your party but most of all go away valuing your ideas and wanting to read your book.

JM: Tell us about your *Author 101* series.

RS: I coauthored *Author 101* with publishing expert Rick Frishman (www.RickFrishman.com), someone I greatly admire. It's an insider's guide to getting published and how to become a smart author.

The book helps maximize opportunities for the benefit of your book's success and shows you how to move through the process of gathering opportunities and increasing your platform, but doing it in a knowledgeable way. You don't start out as a novice, but as a pro in motion with the information you need. Besides becoming an author, which certainly adds credibility to whatever you're trying to share with the public, you want to learn how to do it in a meaningful way.

The *Author 101* series includes four books on everything from writing a book proposal, to finding an agent, to understanding how to create best-selling nonfiction, to publicizing your book, to maximizing your visibility. Every author should read these books because they include the insider secrets behind the scenes of how to become an accomplished author. An author can never know too much about getting published.

START SPREADING THE WORD...

Spreading the word about your book is up to you. Don't rely on your publisher, because I can tell you from experience that if you get any successful publicity out of them, you're lucky.

Here are some ways to start spreading the word about your book:

Tell people about your book project

Talking about your book is useful for a couple of reasons. It puts some pressure on you to actually complete your book, because you've told colleagues, friends and family members that you're working on one. They're likely to be supportive and encouraging, and this positive feedback can help you get through the times when you have difficulties or feel like giving up.

Start small

Write a booklet or special report to give your clients. Start an e-mail newsletter or blog. Get into the habit of writing regularly and also communicating with your customers and clients. After they begin reading your work, if it's good they'll likely be interested in your book when it's completed. The material in your newsletter or special report can become part of your book also, so you're not wasting time and effort. In fact, if you've already written material for presentations or meetings, then you probably have sections of your book already written.

Begin a blog

Starting a blog is an easy way to begin writing your book. It's also a great way to spread the word about your book. You can choose to make it public, or you can keep it private and use the blog simply as a content management system. Services such as TypePad and WordPress are great for this. Organizing your thoughts and ideas into chapters is one of the toughest parts of putting a book together, but a blog makes this amazingly easy. You can write sections of your book as blog posts and easily edit, organize, and move them around later.

Have a Web site.

If you already have a Web site for your business, that's great. If you don't, create a bare-bones site that you can expand and update when your book comes out. What you're trying to do is create as many ways as possible for people to find your book, and a Web site is a necessity for this.

You may want to sell your book from your Web site or link to your book on Amazon or other online retailers, but you'll need a Web site to do so. Also, having a Web site and an e-mail list are considered essential parts of your "platform" that publishers look for when they sign authors.

I recommend GoDaddy (www.GoDaddy.com) for your domain name and Web hosting needs.

CHAPTER 13:

Appearing on Television

"You teach law at NYU for ten years and nobody cares. You get on television, and everybody says, 'There's George!'

George Ross
Trump-Style Negotiation
Donald Trump's Chief Negotiator as Seen On *The Apprentice*

Television is one of the most effective ways to reach the largest possible audience and one of the fastest ways to make yourself, your product or your business famous.

If you've never been on TV before, seek out local programs first. Watch the local talk and news shows in your area to get a sense for what topics they feature and what types of stories the reporters like to cover. Think about how you can pitch yourself and what your "story angle" or "hook" is (something that will get and keep the producer's—and the audience's—attention).

Your goal is to become a celebrity expert in your field who appears frequently on TV. Usually, you'll be identified by your company affiliation or the name of your product, so even if you don't specifically discuss it, you'll still get some publicity. This is another reason you need to have a Web site—so if the program plugs you too quickly or, in the worst-case scenario, not at all, audience members who search for you online can easily find you.

A successful appearance on one program often leads to appearances on other programs (media beget media). Equally important is that with each television appearance, you'll have a clip, which is essential for the day a national program calls and asks to see your other TV appearances.

Insider Interview: Jeff Crilley, Reporter

Jeff Crilley (www.JeffCrilley.com) is an Emmy Award-winning television reporter based in Dallas and author of the book *Free Publicity*. I spoke to Jeff about what producers look for when booking guests and how you can get publicity for your products and services without appearing like a salesperson on TV (a producer's worst nightmare).

JORDAN MCAULEY: What's the best way to approach television producers?

JEFF CRILLEY: You can't just call up a reporter and say, "I run a flower shop." What do you have that's of value to the viewer? That's where most publicity campaigns fall short: They put the spotlight on themselves. Keep the spotlight on the message instead of the messenger.

Here's an example. There are dozens and dozens of flower shops in Dallas. Each year around Valentine's Day, the same one is on TV. Why? The owner is smart and proactive. He knows the television stations are going to do shows on Valentine's Day. So a few weeks before, he starts calling around to the morning shows and talking to producers and reporters and saying, "Valentine's Day is coming up. If you'd like to do a story on one of the busiest days of the year for flowers, we'd be happy to host you." The next thing you know, the small mom-and-pop flower shop ends up on four or five TV channels.

JM: What could a small-business owner say to the producer?

JC: Sometimes it's about talking about your area of expertise, and sometimes it's about your knowledge of how to run a small business.

Simply call the television station and tell the producer, "I know a lot of people watching your TV show have small businesses. Unfortunately, many people will end up losing a lot of money because they go about it all wrong. I'd like to come on your show and talk about the top five mistakes small-business owners make."

JM: If you had to give just one tip about being on TV, what would it be?

JC: Television producers are looking for passion. When you're on the phone with a journalist, it's really an audition for the show because the producer is thinking: "If they're fired up now, just think about how they'll be on TV." So if you're feeling funky or don't have any mojo that day, I wouldn't make that phone call.

You don't have to be over the top, but you should be passionate enough so when people are flipping the channel, they'll say, "Wow, this guy's into it!" Make sure everything is aimed at the value the show is giving their viewers. Don't sound like a commercial."

JM: How should people get their plug across while on TV?

JC: Most television producers understand that plugging your business or product is a give-and-take. They're getting a great guest on their show, while you're getting a plug.

I would ask politely after you're booked, "Is there any way you can put my Web site up on the screen just in case people want to contact me instead of the TV show. That way, they won't have to call your newsroom for any information."

These days, shows are very generous when giving plugs for that very reason. They don't want 200 people calling asking who was just on the show. We usually put up a full screen with the cover of your book along with your Web site, phone number, etc., just so people won't call us.

JM: How should someone prepare to be on TV?

JC: Go through the five questions you can imagine the reporter asking you. Most people don't understand that they actually control the interview—not the anchor, reporter or host. The anchor is running from studio to studio to sit down with a guest and talk to him. They're just trying to fill those three to five minutes and make it interesting. They're depending on you.

This gives you the upper hand so you can talk about what's most important to you and what you're most passionate about. If they ask you a question out of left field, you can say, "That's a very good question, and it reminds me of another good point I want to make." The reporter often doesn't really care about the answer to the question; he or she just wants to fill the time.

JM: Any thoughts on creating segment ideas?

JC: Look for trends in your industry. If something changes or is compelling, or the media hasn't picked up on something yet, call them.

JM: When are the best times to contact television producers?

JC: News is a supply-and-demand business with ebbs and flows. From more than two decades working the street as a reporter, I can tell you that any time around a government holiday is a slow news day. Barring some high-speed chase or double homicide, it's going to be a slow news day.

Judges don't schedule court cases during a holiday. Schools are closed. The stock market is closed. The whole country works the same way—we take holidays. But the news industry can't take holidays. If you want to increase your chances of getting news coverage, approach the media when you're not in competition with anyone.

You can pull out your calendar for the entire year and start circling government holidays. Thanksgiving through New Year's is a very slow season. December is the slowest. All the news makers disappear. Corporate America can't send out press releases or do interviews because everyone's on vacation with the family—but you can, so that's a great time to start pitching.

HOW TO GET ON OPRAH AND OTHER TV SHOWS

An endorsement from one of the most powerful media moguls in the world and tons of follow-up publicity for your product and company are why almost every entrepreneur, author and expert dreams of getting featured in one of Oprah Winfrey's media outlets (*The Oprah Winfrey Show*, *O Magazine*, Oprah & Friends Radio, or OWN: The Oprah Winfrey Network).

There's no reason you shouldn't aim to sit on Oprah's couch, but consider this: Professional athletes don't suddenly show up at the Super

Bowl—they've been practicing for years. Appearing on *Oprah* is like a Broadway debut, so you'll want to get some off-Broadway practice first.

While everyone wants to get on *Oprah*, remember that there are many others TV shows you can get booked on. The tips below apply mostly to *Oprah*, but they are also relevant for other TV talk shows, many of which may actually be better suited for you.

If you're lucky enough to appear as a guest on one of Oprah's programs or if she endorses your product by giving it away, talks about it on her TV or radio show, or writes about it in her magazine, you will suddenly be exposed to a potential audience of 48 million people around the country. That's all good news, right? Yes—as long as you're ready to handle the resulting publicity, manufacturing and distribution that could be the result of this mass attention. So don't underestimate the need to be prepared if you get a call from an *Oprah* producer.

Authors and publishers certainly crave the attention that Oprah gives to books, but they also know that an appearance on the show doesn't ensure a best-seller. When Oprah includes a selection in her book club, the book is almost guaranteed to become a best-seller because Oprah is endorsing it. However, when an author simply appears on an Oprah program, his or her book can have a spike in sales for a day or more, or the show may have minimal impact on sales. However, being able to say, "As Seen on *Oprah*" or "As Seen in *O Magazine*" is what you really want, because that's what will set you apart from your competition.

Expert Interview: Susan Harrow, PR Secrets

Because so many people want to appear on *Oprah*, I went to Susan Harrow (www.MyPRSecrets.com) for advice. In addition to being a media coach and publicity expert, Susan is the author of the *Ultimate Guide to Getting Booked on Oprah* (www.AppearonOprah.com). While Susan's focus in her book is on Oprah's program, her pitching strategies are useful for other TV shows as well.

One of the first pieces of good news that I got from Susan is that getting on *Oprah* is possible, even if you're not a celebrity and you don't have a publicist. As I've suggested throughout this book, with some creativity and ingenuity you can reach almost anyone you want, including Oprah and her producers. Don't stop there, however. You should have a broader campaign aimed at getting you or your product on numerous radio and TV programs, not just one.

Below are eight tips that Susan Harrow offers for getting booked on *Oprah*:

1. Get media training

You'll want to have some media training before you receive a call from an *Oprah* producer. You can't count on advance notice. You may get a phone call and have to fly to Chicago the next day. Don't think about this training just in terms of *Oprah*; think about it for all the other media appearances you'll do in the future, as well.

"Getting on Oprah without media training is like trying to run a marathon without walking a mile," Susan says. "You have to be so fluid in your conversation and be able to speak about your subject with ease when there are bright lights on you, millions of people looking at you, things are changing at the last minute, and it's really frantic."

You have to maintain your composure and remember what you're going to say, say it in a compelling way, and while you're in the middle of a conversation. Typically you're not the only one on a show. It's like being in an Italian family where everybody is talking at once, then they turn to you and say, "Now what do you think?"

2. Watch the show

"Your first step is to record two to four weeks of *Oprah*," notes Susan. "Then sit down in a comfy spot and watch them all at once. This will give you a sense of what's hot on *Oprah* for the next few months, because it changes and goes in cycles. Notice which producers, listed on the credits at the end, are responsible for each particular type of segment. Send the producer information only after you're sure of who you'd like to approach and why."

3. Pitch a hot topic

"Never pitch yourself, your product or your book," warns Susan. "Propose a topic that's relevant to Oprah's audience—controversy, relationships, personal triumph, makeovers—then prove that you're the expert on that topic by telling only the information that's relevant to the idea you're pitching."

4. Put together a winning press kit

"Send your book if you have one; if not, an article will do," recommends Susan. "Also include a pitch or story idea page and a bio paragraph. Be as brief as possible."

5. Explore Oprah's Web site

There's a wealth of information about how to get on the show on Oprah's Web site (www.Oprah.com), including archives going back nearly a decade (search "archives" on the main page) and information about future shows. The Web site's "Be on the Show" section offers upcoming show topics where producers are looking for guests, and how to contact them. There are also message boards and newsgroups all designed to connect you to others with similar interests.

6. Create six dynamic sound bites

"Talk out loud the most important ideas, concepts and points of your topic as they relate to the idea you're pitching," Susan suggests.

7. Know the unwritten rules

If you get a call from a producer asking for more information, know that this is really an audition. You need to have your information in front of you and be able to speak concisely and articulately. The producer is listening to see if you'd make a good guest on TV or not. At the end of the phone call, it's OK to ask the producer if he or she thinks being on the show is a possibility for you or not. If they say "probably not," ask why. That way, you'll at least have a little constructive feedback from an *Oprah* producer.

8. Don't jump to conclusions.

After you speak to a producer, don't jump to conclusions and start telling everyone (or announce on your Web site) that you're going to be on the program. Don't start calling other media outlets telling them you're going to be on *Oprah*. Appearing on another program could actually cause your *Oprah* appearance to be canceled, and if the show is postponed or doesn't air for a while, you could be embarrassed.

"You need to be persistent, and you need to be passionate," advises Susan. "Most of the people who get on *Oprah* are so passionately committed to what they're doing, they don't care if they get on *Oprah* or not. They'll continue to do what they're doing for the rest of their lives or however long it's right for them because it's what they truly believe in. They're not going to stop just because they didn't get on *Oprah*."

Whether it's one of Oprah's producers or another program calling, you need to be ready. You may just be waking up or right in the middle of feeding your child lunch, but the producer doesn't care. Chances are the producer has read about you in another publication, heard you on the radio, or read your pitch letter or e-mail.

Now you have about a minute to make your pitch. You want to be enthusiastic but not overpowering; articulate but not overly rehearsed. Remember, your goal is to convey your expertise and why you would be a good guest for the show they're scheduling. Of course, you're hoping they'll plug your product or business, too, but you shouldn't pitch your product. Hopefully, you'll pass this phone "audition."

HOW TO GET ON REALITY TV

Though they're obviously very different from news and TV talk shows, reality programs also offer an excellent way to get publicity. Think of the contestants on reality TV shows you watch—they're usually introduced by name and where they work or what they do. People who appear on reality television get publicity during the program and after, both on the show and in other media. And, if it's a competition show, you don't have to be the winner. Just being on the show is enough.

Because of the exposure that a reality show gets, there are also a myriad of publicity opportunities after it's over, such as speaking engagements, public appearances, joint ventures and endorsements. For example, Kristi Frank, who appeared on the first season of *The Apprentice*, now speaks at business seminars and was hired by "millionaire maker" Dan Kennedy (www.DanKennedyPresents.com) to help promote the latest titles in his *No B.S. Books* (www.NoBSBooks.com) series.

Almost all reality television shows today are built around experts. If you think your company, product or location would be a good fit for a reality TV show, contact some reality TV producers. The company that produced the show is usually listed in the program's credits. Then just do an online search to locate the company's contact information and write a short pitch letter. Because the season you're watching has already been taped, suggest a good match for the season "in production." That will show the producer that you're realistic and know what you're talking about. Be sure to include all your contact information.

Expert Interview: Brian Patrick Flynn, Designer

Brian Patrick Flynn (www.BrianPatrickFlynn.com), designer and on-air talent for TBS' *Movie and a Makeover*, offers these tips for small businesses that want to get a product on popular interior design and home shows such as *Extreme Home Makeover* and the programs on HGTV:

JORDAN MCAULEY: Why do designers choose to put donated and/or discounted products on shows?

BRIAN PATRICK FLYNN: Every show uses fast, affordable, accessible places like IKEA (www.IKEA.com) to get most of their stuff. But if I'm designing a Mediterranean-inspired great room, for example, and you're a Mediterranean style designer with original sofas that fit my aesthetic, I'd rather put your sofa in my program because it's new and more fresh than what viewers have already seen. It gives the show a more solid design concept and shows that your product is an integral part of the designer's vision.

JM: What are the benefits to the business?

BPF: One benefit is that your product will look really good because I'll design a room that really showcases it well. Two, you not only get exposure to tons of viewers, but you also get a natural endorsement because the designer wouldn't actually use the product unless he or she truly loved it. You don't get that when you advertise.

JM: Who should people contact at a show?

BPF: You should get your press kit mentioning your Web site to the production manager, and/or look-books and samples to the on-air talent. The production manager is in charge of accounts payable and receivable, so one of his or her jobs is to save money on the production. If they can get a promotional agreement for the show, they can now save on the budget for materials because they have a source that can supply them in exchange for the exposure. The talent, like myself, wants to design the best-looking space available, so if I love your work I'll naturally be inclined to want to share it with my audience.

JM: What's the most important thing people should remember?

BPF: The most important thing for me is to see high-quality photos of your product, preferably on a Web site. When people invest in great photography, it speaks volumes about the quality of the product. I also need to know exact dimensions, whether it's a lamp or it's fashion, because I need to make sure it will fit to scale.

JM: What are some other tips for getting products on the air?

BPF: One secret is to offer specific prices for designers. Say you design chandeliers and they're normally $5,000 each. If you offer one to me at cost for $1,700, anticipating I'll incorporate it into one of my designs,

I'll probably want to use it. If it makes the space look stellar, I'm going to be more inclined to come back and purchase something else of yours. I'm always trying to get high-end looks regardless of my budget. So, if your product made my $4,000 project look like a $50,000 project, I'm very likely to use that product again.

You aren't really losing anything by offering TV designers great price breaks or donated products, because you make every dollar back with the exposure you get in trade. Even if you could buy an ad for that, you wouldn't get the benefits of an endorsement from the show.

RESOURCES

If you want to appear on reality TV as a star or contestant, visit the site of the show you're interested in and occasionally check for casting calls. There are also several Web sites that focus specifically on reality TV castings:

Reality TV Casting Call

www.RealityTVCastingCall.com

This Web site includes casting notices for many programs and offers an e-mail notification service for casting calls.

Reality Wanted

www.RealityWanted.com

By registering (free) at this site, you provide your contact information to casting agents and others looking to cast their reality TV program.

Reality TV Web site

www.RealityTVWebSite.com

This Web site lists all the reality shows along with links to their Web sites, plus descriptions of what type of guests the shows are looking for. As of this writing, *Trading Spaces* was seeking neighbors while *The Amazing Race* was taking applications for its coming season.

HOW TO GET ON QVC

Who wouldn't want to get on QVC? This home shopping channel broadcasts 24 hours a day to more than 140 million people in four countries (U.S., U.K., Germany, Japan) and features more than 250 new products every week. To find out how to get on QVC, I sought out a QVC expert who has appeared on the channel multiple times.

Insider Interview: Nick Romer, Sell On Q

Nick Romer (www.SellOnQ.com) is an award-winning inventor of more than 100 products for crafters and hobbyists. He is the author of the book *Make Millions Selling on QVC* and has appeared on QVC in the United States for more than 14 years. Nick's products have also been featured on QVC United Kingdom and QVC Germany. He is a recipient of QVC's Million Dollar Sales Award. His innovative products have been sold in more than 22,000 stores in 23 countries and can be found on his Web sites, www.GreenSneakers.com and www.ScrapWow.com.

JORDAN MCAULEY: What's the best way to submit a product to QVC?

NICK ROMER: The best way to get on that requires the least amount of effort is to go to their Web site, www.QVCProductSearch.com, and fill out the online product submission form. You can also send your product to them if you feel it's essential, along with your application. I know this approach has worked for some, but I'm not convinced it's the best way. I believe in the personal touch.

I encourage people to attend a QVC open call. Go to the QVC Web site and look for a QVC Product Search Event. In the past, these events have included its "50 in 50 Tour" where they visited 50 states in 50 days looking for new items. With this approach, you'll increase your chances of getting in front of decision-makers where they'll be able to see and feel your passion while interacting with you about your product.

JM: Many people show up at these open calls. If your product isn't selected, should you give up?

NR: No. I believe the very best way to get on QVC is to use an agent. These agents spend a lot of time reviewing and looking for the best products to bring to QVC. They know the rules of the game. They know a lot of buyers and producers as well as manufacturers. Agents are generally well-connected individuals with keen eyes and ears that can benefit your business in more ways than one.

JM: What should you look for in a QVC agent?

NR: In my opinion, a good QVC agent has a long-standing relationship with QVC of at least five years with multiple, successful products. He or she lives and has an office near QVC [located in West Chester, Pa., in the suburbs of Philadelphia]. He or she should be able to provide a list of current or past clients that you can speak with about their experience. A good agent is also one who focuses the majority of his or her efforts on representing products to QVC.

JM: What are the financial arrangements of using an agent?

NR: The agent should charge between 5% and 10% of the wholesale selling price to QVC and also should be paid only after you receive payment from QVC.

JM: After you know QVC is interested in your product, how do you prepare so that your meeting is successful?

NR: This is an important point. I'm often asked about this, and I cannot stress enough the value of doing your homework. First of all, if your product is unproven, you should test it. See if you can sell it to the public before trying to get it on QVC. Try a consumer trade show or a local fair first. If it doesn't sell at these venues, it probably won't sell on QVC. On the other hand, if your product is already selling well to the public, know why it's selling and build that information into your pitch to prospective agents and QVC buyers.

Another important point is to do your research on other products that are similar. Find out if QVC has been selling this type of product or anything similar before by dong a simple search on its Web site. Their Web site doesn't include products no longer being sold, but at least you can find out if QVC is currently selling something similar.

If QVC is featuring an item similar to yours, you'll have to distinguish your product from the existing product. This can be done in a number of ways, such as price or quality. But if your product is identical, you might have to go back to the drawing board and build in a new twist.

JM: When making your presentation, what should you focus on?

NR: In addition to presenting in terms of benefits [vs. features], it's important to understand what makes QVC successful. QVC stands for Quality, Value and Convenience. If you don't address these issues, whether directly or indirectly in your meetings with the buyers or with agents, you may be left wondering why they haven't accepted your product. They are first in the home-shopping business for many reasons, and these three letters are credited for much of their success.

JM: If your product is accepted by QVC, what happens?

NR: Take a deep breath— this is when the real work begins. After your product has been chosen, you'll start dealing with manufacturing, shipping, pricing and quality assurance. You'll also have decisions to make concerning the on-air presentation of your product. All of these are important considerations, so you have to remain patient and try to enlist your friends and family to help you out.

When you become a QVC vendor for the first time, you receive a welcome packet with a lot of information. The other component that you'll be privy to is access to QVC's vendor Web site. There you'll find everything you're required to know from a technical aspect—guidelines for shipping, product labeling, packaging, invoicing information, product descriptions, preferred vendor lists for shipping, and bar code label creation information. This isn't available to the general public. You'll be able to check on inventory, sales stats, purchase orders, payments made by QVC, and so on. It's the central hub where you'll find most of your answers.

JM: What about your actual appearance on QVC? If you don't have experience in this medium, what should you do?

NR: QVC requires every new on-air salesperson to attend a Guest Excellence Seminar. It's a two-part training program that provides you with a foundation for your on-air appearance. The first part is completed online from home. The second part is an all-day event that takes place at their headquarters.

The training covers QVC's sales philosophy and provides often-overlooked details on where to go for support, what to do when you arrive the day of your airing, general protocol, and legal and claims requirements. Participants also fine tune their product pitches with the help of others in the group before working with one of the actual QVC hosts in a taped mock television presentation. Afterward, a TV sales mentor will discuss your performance with you.

Another option is to hire on-air talent. Someone else might be better suited to present your products on the air, and your contacts at QVC might be able to assist you in finding the right person.

JM: You believe people should practice ahead of time. What specific tactics do you recommend?

NR: The format of QVC is time-limited, so it's important to prepare for a short demo. A good way of doing this is to develop three key points about your product. Of course, you can deviate and expand, but having three key points provides for a strong foundation for both you and the host. It also keeps things simple for the viewers, making them more likely to make a purchase.

A NOTE ABOUT HSN (HOME SHOPPING NETWORK)

Though it reaches a smaller audience than QVC, HSN (ww.HSN.com) is a home-shopping channel seen in the U.S. on cable and satellite. Many of the tips for getting on QVC apply to the Home Shopping Network also. You can find details for submitting your product to HSN on its Web site under "Becoming an HSN Partner."

Study Your Options

The world of television is vast. It's important, therefore, that you get to know the shows that make the best sense for your media exposure. If you haven't been watching TV and want to be on it, start tuning in now. When you get a hunch that approaching a particular show would be a smart move, watch the program regularly. Notice the types of segments, as well as the names and personalities of the people in front of the camera. Sometimes, credits at the end of the show will list segment producers. If not, check the Web site or call the show for the producers' names.

CHAPTER 14

Creating Press Kits and Press Releases

"A terrible thing happens without publicity—nothing."

P.T. Barnum
There's a Customer Born Every Minute
Joe Vitale & Jeffrey Gitomer

Although the way press releases are distributed has changed (they're now often online), they remain one of the most important elements in a publicity campaign. Paul Hartunian (www.Hartunian.com) is one of the world's top experts in writing star-powered press releases. Here, Paul shares his strategy for writing a killer press release:

"I've seen so much bad advice on the Internet about how to write a press release. Not only can this waste a ton of time and money, it can also affect your standing with reporters. If you keep sending out lousy press releases, if you don't play the game according to the media's rules, you'll get a reputation as someone who doesn't know what they're doing. Reporters will avoid you in droves.

There are rules you should NEVER violate. I don't care what the other so-called publicity experts say, or those $20 books on publicity you see in the bookstores and libraries.

- **Press releases should be one page and one page only.** If you can't tell your story in one page, you don't know what you're talking about.

- **Your release should be on 8½-by-11-inch paper only.** No odd sizes. No special shapes. No "original designs." Outside the U.S., use the standard paper size for the country.

- **You must use plain white paper.** No letterhead, printed borders or photographs. No other color, tint or shade. Absolutely nothing but plain, white paper.

- **Your press release must be double spaced.** Never single space the entire body copy. This is probably the top reason that reporters toss out press releases. Single spacing screams to the media that you don't know how to play the game.

Now, let me give you some tips on what should go on this one-page press release.

In the upper left corner, you only have two options. Choose the one that's more appropriate for your purpose. The first option is to put the words "For Immediate Release" in that corner. You've probably seen these words before, but you may not know their purpose. These three words do two things for you and the reporter. First they tell the reporter that he can use your information whenever he or she wishes. Today, tomorrow, next month, next year, whenever.

"For Immediate Release" does something even more important, however. When you put these three words in the upper-left corner of your press release, you're letting the reporter know that you know how to play the publicity game. The more clues like that you include in your press release, the more confidence the reporter will have in you.

The only other option for the upper-left corner is what I've termed a "time qualifier." A time qualifier tells the reporter exactly when—and when not—to use your release. Let's say you're putting together a release about Father's Day. In the upper-left corner, you would put "For Release On or Before Father's Day." Not only are you telling the reporter exactly when to use your release, you're again giving him a signal that you know how to play the game. Not many press releases have time qualifiers. So if you use one the right way, you score big points with the reporter.

Now let's look at the upper-right corner of your press release. There you only have one option. You're going to put these exact words in the upper-right corner of every release you ever write: "For Further Information, Contact:". On the second line in the upper-right corner, you're going to put the name and direct phone number of a real, live human being. You're not going to just put the name of a company, organization, etc. (If you do that, you'll scream to the reporter that you probably don't know how to play the publicity game.) So, on that second line, I'd put "Paul Hartunian - (973-857-4142).

Now let's look at the headline. The headline of a press release has one job only: to force the reporter to keep reading. Don't force your press release headline to do anything more than that. You don't need any special skills to write a great headline. You should use a formula headline for your release. There are hundreds of tried, tested formula headlines. One example is "New Product Offers Benefit."

Let's move onto the body copy of your release. The body copy has three parts. In Part One, you tell your whole story in two or three sentences—and I mean that literally. If you can't tell your entire story in two or three sentences, you don't know what you're talking about, and you'll tell reporters that you can't get to the point.

For example, I can tell you the history of the Revolutionary War in two sentences:

1. We fought the British.

2. They lost.

If I can tell you the history of the Revolutionary War that quickly, you can tell me your story in two sentences.

Part Two of your press release should contain quotes from you, along with your credentials. Always quote yourself. Never quote anyone else. Why give someone else any attention in your press release? It's *your* release. If someone else wants attention, let them write their own release.

Part Three of your press release should contain your call to action. What do you want to happen as a result of your press release?

Throughout your press release, you must use what I call the "Who Cares Style of Writing." After every sentence you write, read it out loud and ask, "Who cares?" If you can't answer, it's a lousy sentence.

Let me give you a couple of examples of lousy headlines that don't pass the "who cares?" test.

"Janice Jones Promoted to Vice President of Sales"

Who cares that Janice Jones was promoted to vice president of sales? No one cares. Not even Janice Jones. She didn't get a raise—she just got more work.

"Allied Manufacturing Announces 35% Increase In Sales"

Do you care that Allied Manufacturing had a 35% increase in sales? I doubt it. Who cares?

Get the idea? Be sure every sentence you write in your press release passes the "who cares?" test.

A successful publicity campaign includes two more pieces of paper: the bio and the Q&A. The vast majority of people trying to get publicity don't know to include them or how to write them.

Never send a press release without also having a bio and Q&A ready to go. Without them, you'll almost certainly waste your time trying to get the publicity that will mean dollars in your bank account. After all, aren't those dollars the ultimate reason you want publicity?

If you'd like to learn how to run your own publicity campaigns locally or nationwide for less than $10, go to www.MillionDollarPublicity.com.

Do you need story ideas for your press releases? Go to www.101WaysToGetPublicity.com.

Would you like a whole slew of ready-to-go press releases, headlines, opening paragraphs, and story ideas specifically written for your business, profession or industry? Go to www.NichePublicityManuals.com.

Publicity has given me—and many others—everything I've wanted in life. It's also given me one of the things I value most: my freedom. I want you to have the same opportunity.

"CELEBRITY-IZING" YOUR PRESS RELEASES

There are many ways you can use celebrities in your press releases (or at least link to them). Here are my favorites:

Link your press release to celebrity news.
"Hypnotic marketing" expert Joe Vitale (www.MrFire.com), author of *The Attractor Factor* and contributor to *The Secret*, often uses celebrities in his press releases. This is one reason he's been so successful. Here, Joe shares advice about how to do it:

"When I was promoting my course, *Hypnotic Marketing Secrets* (www.MyHypnoticMarketing.com), I was trying to think of different ways to drive traffic to it. One night I was watching television, and I saw a commercial with Britney Spears promoting a new perfume she was endorsing. It was fairly mesmerizing.

"I started writing a press release that said: 'Britney Spears Accused of Using Hypnotic Marketing Secrets in Her New TV Ad.' This was very legitimate, because I—as a hypnotic marketer, hypnotic writer, hypnotic salesperson—had a whole package of hypnotic selling secrets. So I commented on her marketing efforts. I also associated myself with a celebrity.

"This was all truthful—I just tied it into something that was going on. Now of course I was piggybacking off of a HUGE name. When I sent out that press release, a whole lot of people who were Googling 'Britney Spears' saw it. And when they read it, they learned about me.

"Suddenly, tens of thousands of new people—not just on the Internet, but offline as well—were aware of me, my product, my service, and everything I was doing. When I did my next teleseminar about a week or two after that news release went out about *Hypnotic Marketing Secrets*, we had record-breaking numbers of people come on who heard me speak about how Britney Spears was using and misusing them.

"This was publicity; this was thinking in a bigger way; and in this case, I was taking a ride off the fame of Britney Spears. People searching for her name suddenly saw my name associated with hers, and a whole new audience became aware of me."

Joan Stewart, editor of *The Publicity Hound* (www.PublicityHound.com), offered me this story about one of her clients:

"For years, Debra Holtzman (www.TheSafetyExpert.com) kept wishing and hoping that she'd generate publicity in top-tier newspapers and magazines and on the big morning TV shows like *Good Morning America*. A mother of two who's also an attorney, Debra is a one of the foremost experts on child safety. But the wishing and hoping didn't do much good. Then Debra found the key that not only unlocked the door to publicity but had the media practically tripping over themselves to interview her. She ties her expertise to celebrities—sometimes several times a month. It all depends on how much material the stars feed her. And feed her they do.

"On May 17, 2006, when celebrity magazines printed a photograph showing Britney Spears driving in her convertible, with 8-month-old son Sean Preston in the back, sitting in a car seat facing forward, slumped over to one side, Debra wrote a press release titled, 'Britney Spears Needs Baby Safety Training!'"

She posted it at ExpertClick.com, the subscription-based Web site that serves as a data base of experts for the media and lets subscribers post up to 52 press releases a year. The story was picked up by celebrity gossip bloggers and top-tier media outlets.

That same month, when Angelina Jolie and Brad Pitt welcomed their baby girl, Shiloh Nouvel Jolie-Pitt, Debra swung into action and issued a press release with the headline, "Angelina and Brad's Perfect Baby Room for Shiloh." It described some of the dangers of a baby's nursery and included a checklist of eleven tips on how the couple could keep the baby safe.

Also that month, with the paparazzi on his trail, Pitt went for a bicycle ride in Langstrand, Namibia, with son Maddox Jolie-Pitt, 4, and daughter Zahara Jolie-Pitt, 16 months. Maddox, who wore a helmet, pedaled a tricycle. Zahara rode in a blue papoose strapped to

Brad's back. As soon as the photos hit the newsstands, Debra swung into action. She wrote a press release about the danger of riding with a baby on a bike. "(Zahara) needs a helmet and closed-toe shoes," she told *Us Weekly*. "I highly recommend toddlers ride in a child trailer pulled by a bike. It's more stable and secure."

On Aug. 1, 2006, just after Mel Gibson's drunken driving arrest, Debra issued a release titled "Top 10 Tips to Drive Like a Star, But Not Mel Gibson." On Sept. 4, 2006, just after "Crocodile Hunter" Steve Irwin was killed by a stingray while snorkeling, Debra posted another press release on ExpertClick.com: "Teach Children How to Be Safe Around Pets and Wild Animals." She didn't name Irwin or mention the incident in the release. However, journalists and anyone else who was searching online for information on that news story probably would have found her press release in the list of "organic" search results.

All those releases mean more sales of Debra's books, *The Panic-Proof Parent* and *The Safe Baby*, which she mentions in the releases. Her expertise as a child safety expert, and all those press releases that tie into celebrities, are responsible for Debra's being quoted in papers such as *USA Today* and *The New York Times* and bookings for guest appearances on shows such as *Today*. She has a long list of media hits on her Web site, The SafetyExpert.com.

Joan Stewart says others can use that same piggybacking approach in their own press releases. She notes that "half the work is just keeping your ears open for opportunities."

Tie your press release to a popular movie or TV show

This is one of my favorite strategies, and it can work equally well whether you're based in Boise or the Big Apple. One of the most-watched TV programs, especially among women, is *Desperate House-*

wives, because so many viewers identify with the housewives and their problems. So if your target market is women, why not stage an event based on *Desperate Housewives* (or similar show)?

Think about what other TV shows people talk about at the water cooler. As the famous copywriter Robert Collier once said, you want to "enter the conversation already in their minds." Any number of businesses, from dentists to hairdressers, could offer *Ugly Betty* promotions, *Next Top Model* makeovers, *Project Runway* wardrobe consultations, etc. Travel agencies could create a *Lost* adventure vacation to an exotic island, a getaway to Los Angeles called *The Hills*, a *Nip/Tuck* vacation to Miami, or a *Damages* trip to New York City.

Here's an example of a successful tie-in to the TV show *Survivor*. In 2001, Cold Stone Creamery (www.ColdStoneCreamery.com) ice cream decided to hold a limited-time *Survivor* promotion. Because contestants on the show are often forced to eat bugs to "survive," Cold Stone's customers were offered chocolate-covered crickets as a mix-in at 142 of the company's locations. Doug Ducey, Cold Stone's CEO, said every location sold out of the crickets the first week, even though the supply was expected to last a month. Cold Stone's sales rose 8 percent that summer, and after the promotion the company received publicity on CBS's *The Early Show*. The hosts even tasted the crickets.

Name something after a star

Restaurants and diners often name sandwiches after stars. L.A.'s famous Pink's Hot Dogs (www.PinksHollywood.com) names its hot dogs after famous celebrities. Sometimes they even ask a star to create a signature hot dog, then name it after the star. Some of the items on Pink's menu are a "Martha Stewart Dog" (with relish, onions, bacon, chopped tomatoes, sauerkraut and sour cream), a "Rosie O'Donnell Long Island Dog" (with mustard, onions, chili and sauerkraut), and an "Ozzy Spice Dog" (with nacho cheese, grilled onions, guacamole and chopped tomatoes). You can name items after popular movies, as well. Starfish Sushi's (StarFishAtlanta.com) menu offers a *Memoirs of a Geisha* roll, an *Ocean's Eleven* roll, an *X-Men* roll, and more.

To get publicity, hold a contest where you ask diners to create and name an item after a star, then ask patrons to vote and choose the winner. Or host an "all-you-can-eat" contest with selected items named after stars or movies from your menu. Of course, let the media know about these events with a star-powered press release.

Give a celebrity an award

Create an award based on your business, and then choose a celebrity to be "best" or "worst." Best teeth, best hair, best body, etc., always works. Be sure to choose a celebrity who's constantly in the news or tabloids. Dermatologist Dr. Vail Reese (www.UnionSquareDerm.com) lists celebrities each year with the worst skin and the best skin. When Britney Spears was publicly rushed to the hospital in an ambulance after her apparent breakdown, Dr. Reese sent out a press release naming Spears as having the "worst skin in Hollywood." Because of the intense Britney coverage at this time, this "award" made national news.

Beverly Malone, author of *Whatever! A Baby Boomer's Journey into Middle Age*, began a campaign to bring attention to her new Web site, EnjoyYourMenopause.com. She named Natalie Cole as a member of her Baby Boomer Diva Web Hall of Fame. Web site traffic and product sales increased after that award. The Diva Web Hall of Fame now includes a mix of celebrities such as Madonna, Whoopi Goldberg, Diane Keaton, Roseanne Barr, Vanessa Williams and Reba McEntire, as well as ordinary women.

Create a "Top 10" list

The late Mr. Blackwell created the well-known "Worst Dressed" list of Hollywood stars. *Autograph* magazine creates a "Top 10 Best & Worst Signers" list each year that always gets a lot of attention, often nationally covered by the Associated Press. ContactAnyCelebrity.com creates a "Most Wanted Celebrities" list each year naming celebrities who are most sought out by fans, businesses, nonprofits and the media. You get the idea.

Insider Interview: Drew Gerber, Wasabi Publicity

Wasabi Publicity (www.WasabiPublicity.com) is one of the country's top virtual PR firms. I spoke with the company's cofounder, Drew Gerber, about how to maximize your press kit. You can also use Wasabi's Press Kit 24/7 service (www.MyPressKit247.com) to put your press kit online.

JORDAN MCAULEY: What is the importance of having a press kit?

DREW GERBER: The main advantage is that this is your first opportunity to make a great impression with the media. It's how you introduce yourself and have the media decide whether they're going to actually cover you or not.

JM: What are some of the advantages of having your press kit online?

DG: A recent survey found that 93 percent of the media prefer to get their information via an online press kit. The reason for this is that in the fast-paced media world, they're working 24/7. With an online press kit, they can have all the information they need to do a story on you right there at their fingertips anytime they want it.

JM: What's the best way to let a reporter know about your online press kit?

DG: From everything I've heard, it's a reporter's pet peeve to receive unsolicited hard-copy press kits. As a PR company, we never send an unsolicited press kit. I strongly recommend that no one ever do that. Instead, let the reporter know about your online press kit with an e-mail.

JM: Do reporters mind getting unsolicited e-mail?

DG: Not if you have a relevant story idea. We're usually dealing with national high-level media. Local is a different story, because they don't get nearly the volume of pitches. So if you want to do local media, then I think you're fine sending unsolicited hard-copy press kits to them.

JM: Should one personalize these e-mails or send a mass e-mail to a list of reporters?

DG: Personalize it. If you're pitching the *Today* show, make sure you know something about the producer you're pitching and make it relevant to what he or she does. Another pet peeve of the media that they cannot stand is when you're pitching one reporter and that person doesn't even cover that beat.

JM: Any tips for picking a PR firm that's going to really help you get coverage instead of just taking your money?

DG: When looking for a PR company, I always recommend that you ask, "What are some recent media placements that you've gotten your clients?" Then you actually see if those are the types of placements that you want. Last month, our PR firm got 190 media placements. What I can do is show the client and say, "Is this the type of media placements that you're looking for?"

Something that's unique about us is that we're an "open book" PR company. Every month, you get a report from us that outlines everything we did for you. You know all the outreach, you know all the work that's been done, and you can actually look and see if this was worth the money.

I don't recommend getting locked into contracts. We don't do contracts at Wasabi. Most clients stay with us for a very long time, so there's really no need for a contract.

WHAT TO HAVE IN YOUR ONLINE PRESS KIT

Drew Gerber of Wasabi Publicity (www.WasabiPublicity.com) and Press Kit 24/7 (www.MyPressKit247.com) recommends the following elements for your online press kit:

1. **Welcome or Home Page.** This page should clearly and concisely describe exactly who you are and what you do. "It's like your elevator pitch or your book," says Drew. "It needs to grab their attention right off the bat."

2. **Bio/About You.** "Give them the meat of who your clients are—companies or nonprofits," Drew explains.

3. **Images.** This allows the media person to go to your online press kit and download images if they want to use them for the story. Drew recommends having multiple formal shots of the key person, plus "some fun shots and an action shot" of them.

4. **News Angles/News Stories/Story Ideas.** This gives the media ideas of how they could actually use you in a story.

5. **Questions to Ask.** "This is more important for broadcast than it is for print," Drew says. "Print reporters consider themselves more hard-core reporters than broadcast does. For radio and TV, we always give them a list of questions."

6. **Products.** If you have products, Drew says to put product images on there.

7. **Testimonials or Usable Quotes.** "When a reporter is doing a story in the middle of the night and they need a quote from you, they can go to the online press kit," Drew notes. He suggests providing five or ten usable quotes that they can place right into their story.

For an easy way to put your press kit online in a format the media will love, visit Press Kit 24/7 (www.MyPressKit247.com).

MEDIA EXPOSURE + CELEBRITY LEVERAGE = POWERFUL PUBLICITY

The media have the power to propel a business out of obscurity into prominence. This chapter has shown you how to tap into that power to make your business and yourself a star. The method? Making the most of the media attention you get. Use these ideas well, and soon you'll have a rocking publicity campaign.

CHAPTER 15

Getting Coverage in Magazines & Newspapers

"Like any Hollywood starlet, Pinkberry knew it had arrived when it made the pages of two of America's most popular publications, *Us Weekly* and *People*. Forget the country's best yogurt—this is its most famous."

Fast Company

Because it's generally more difficult to land a spot in national publications, it's smart to first focus on local ones. Free local weeklies are viable outlets because they are often eager for editorial content. Contact some local publications and volunteer to write a column. Think out of the box. If you're a physician, you could write a column that covers topics such as seasonal allergies, tips to keep kids healthy at school, how to treat a cold, etc. If you own a computer repair service, you might write about common software and hardware mishaps.

Editors really want to see two things: that you can write, and that you turn your columns in on time. You don't need to be Ernest Hemingway or F. Scott Fitzgerald. All you need to be able to do is share valuable content with the publication's readers. Most magazines and newspapers will print a byline under the title of your column or article. For example, my byline reads "Jordan McAuley is the Founder and President of Contact Any Celebrity at www.ContactAnyCelebrity.com, a service that helps businesses, nonprofits, authors, and the media contact more than 55,000 celebrities and public figures worldwide." Be sure your editor agrees to include your byline before you start writing. Include it with every column or article you send in so they don't forget to add it in the rush of a deadline

I wrote a column for a small, local publication; then, after a year, I approached a larger one. The first magazine I wrote for wanted to see two or three writing samples. But when I approached the larger-circulation magazine and asked how many writing samples to provide, the editor said, "You've been published, don't worry about it." It was that easy. And at both publications, all it took was a simple e-mail to the editors stating that I would like to write for them. After another year, I approached national magazines. They were a little pickier about what they chose to publish, but I landed several writing assignments for magazines with large, six-figure circulations.

In addition to a local column, think about pitching your company's story or another article idea to the business section of your local newspaper, your city's Chamber of Commerce newsletter, your city's business journal, or your college alumni magazine. You might also want to try writing for your industry's trade publication.

Writing columns or articles will probably take some time, but you may already have some of the content. If you publish a newsletter—e-mail or print—you can repurpose those. The same goes for your blog, speeches, book, etc.

To determine the best person to contact about writing for a magazine or newspaper, simply pick up a copy of the publication and look at the masthead for the editor's name. Some publications even feature the editor's name and e-mail address on their Web site.

WHAT ABOUT CELEBRITY MAGAZINES?

Melanie Bromley, *Us Weekly's* Los Angeles bureau chief, says: "The key to coverage is a celebrity tie-in. Without that, we just can't cover it. My pet peeve is pitches that don't have a celebrity tie-in."

Insider Interview: Amy Stumpf, Gift List Media

Amy Stumpf founded Gift List Media (www.MyGiftListMedia.com), a service that helps companies get their products featured in magazine gift guides and on TV. I recently spoke with Amy about how to generate coverage for your product in celebrity magazine gift guides such as in *People, Us Weekly, InStyle,* etc.

JORDAN MCAULEY: What exactly are magazine gift guides?

AMY STUMPF: National women's glossies and celebrity weeklies will often dedicate a huge number of pages to a holiday gift guide. These are great gifts under $100, great gifts for mom, dad, grandparents, teachers, babysitters, kids, etc. For the most part, you can guarantee that a holiday gift guide is going to feature an image. That's the great thing—it's more than just a product mention. They actually show the product's image and where to buy it right there, instead of the usual slot in the back of the magazine.

JM: How does Gift List Media Work?

AS: We distill down the 30,000 contacts of people who work in media. I have ten people doing calls all year to put the information into one consolidated data base. With all the details that we've included, you now have more time to focus on the people who are going to be your best-bet editors, based on the product you're pitching at that time.

JM: What information do you provide?

AS: We list the product categories, like whether it's a traditional holiday gift guide, something more seasonal, or a regular product review column. We find out as much as we can. We know people want to find a good way to present the editors with information that they really want and need at that time, and that's the trick—getting the right pitch to the right editor.

We also list the editor's contact information, the publication's circulation, the feature focus they're looking for at the time, and what they look for year-round. Then we give you contact hints. Everyone has their preferences of how they like to be contacted—whether it's an online press kit or a hard copy in the mail, the best time to reach them on the phone, their pet peeves, etc.

JM: Can businesses that are not name brands get into gift guides?

AS: I think this is going to be the decade of the entrepreneur. Magazine readers and subscribers don't want to see the same products mentioned in issue after issue, month after month. If you're a new company or a small one and can really play up the fact that you're not in every retail establishment, then there's a uniqueness to your product. The challenge is getting your product to the editors who want to see it. That's where we come in.

JM: How do companies submit their products to the magazine?

AS: You need to have a targeted pitch letter and press release. Both should be short and to the point and very specific to the outlet and editor you're pitching. You don't want to send the editor searching for basic facts like contact and pricing information. It needs to be clear and under one page.

It's also worth investing in good quality product shots with and without models, depending on your product. I don't recommend attaching a whole bunch of images to an e-mail, but you should definitely have a section on your Web site where you have your press releases, clips, story ideas, downloadable images, etc.

If you have all of these things—pitch letter, press release, product shots—then you should approach the editor by e-mail. It buys you a little time, too, so you can hold something back and then have more to offer in your follow-up. You can say, "I also have these story ideas and I wanted to share with you a few quotes" or whatever you have. You always want to hold something back because you never want to follow up with just, "I'm calling to see if you got my e-mail."

JM: When should someone start pitching?

AS: You need to first look at which publications are long-lead publications. You need to allow several months in advance, because the gift guides do go through extra editorial processes in-house, and there's more than one person who's in charge. For example, if you start at the beginning of June, you could start with the long-lead magazines and work your way through to the shorter-lead magazines like local parenting and fitness publications. This would take you from June to December.

CHAPTER 16

Getting On Local and National Radio

"There's no limit to the ways you can get into the press. One of the best ways is to become famous for the services you do for the community. There are lots of strategies you can use to do that. You could sponsor a local team. You could put on a charity event. You could do a good turn for someone in the community who needs it."

Paul Hartunian
Million Dollar Publicity Letter
www.Hartunian.com

Although you may think television is a more "glamorous" medium, radio remains a very potent outlet for guests whose goal is to promote something. From the guest's viewpoint, going on a radio show can be less of a hassle; you can be at home or in your office and call in to the station to do the interview.

You still have to prepare your pitch—just as you would for TV—but you don't have the added worries of what to wear and how to appear. You could be in your underwear or pajamas, and no one would know.

Insider Interview: Alex Carroll, Radio Publicity

Alex Carroll (www.RadioPublicity.com) is one of the foremost experts today on getting free radio publicity. He's appeared on more than 1,400 radio shows and sold more than $1.5 million worth of his books on how to beat speeding tickets—*Beat the Cops* and *Speeding Excuses that Work*.

I spoke with Alex about how to get free radio publicity. To find out how to beat speeding tickets, you'll have to read his book.

JORDAN MCAULEY: What's the first step to getting on the radio?

ALEX CARROLL: It's all about giving the listeners a good show. Radio producers know you're selling something, but you've got to give them a good show, and in exchange, you get a plug. That's basically the deal.

There are 10,000 guest spots open every day in America on radio stations across the country. Every day, day in and day out, there is a never-ending demand for guests. Most guests suck, so if you're any good, you'll be in demand.

JM: What are the benefits of getting on the radio?

AC: On radio shows, you get a lot of time to talk. The average television interview is about three minutes. You don't get much time to talk on TV. Plus, it's almost always taped. With radio, you don't have to travel, you don't have to go anywhere, you don't have to dress up, you don't have to worry about stage fright, you don't have to worry about somebody sticking a camera in front of your face.

Print is funny. There's a long delay, then usually what happens is they just mention you in an article as opposed to doing a feature piece about you. Print people also have a tendency to not give your Web site or toll-free number a plug. They just edit that out and you don't have much control. On the radio, you have control because if they say, "Alex, thanks for being on the show," you just butt in and say, "Hey, can I give out my Web site and toll-free number?" You can't do that with print.

Plus, radio reaches more people than any other type of media. Ninety-six percent of the U.S. population listens to radio every week. Seventy-five percent listens to it every day. They're stuck in their cars. It's the only type of media that reaches people at work and in their cars.

JM: What are some of the best ways to get on the radio?

AC: There are four main ways. First, you can hire a PR firm. Hiring a PR firm is a good choice if you have a lot of money and don't have a lot of time. But if you're going to hire a PR firm, be sure to hire a good one. Don't hire some schlocky piece-of-crap PR firm out in the middle of nowhere. You're hiring their contacts. If they don't have any contacts, they're no good to you whatsoever because you can get on the phone and make the contacts just as easily yourself.

The best way to get radio interviews is to advertise in publications that feature guests. Radio Television Interview Report (www.RTIR.com) is the biggest and the best. If you're going to go that route, it's a great way to go. You put your ad in, and the stations call you. You don't have to get on the phone and cold-call. So, if you don't like cold-calling, it's a great thing.

Also, they write the ad for you. They come up with the show pitch and the show idea and that's a challenge. They're really good at coming up with show hooks and show ideas because they've been doing it for twenty years.

The third way is to send out a mass fax or e-mail blast. But radio is an auditory medium. That means they want to hear you. Can they hear your fax? No, except for maybe landing in a trash can.

The last way to get on the radio is by calling and pitching yourself—that's what I do.

7 THINGS YOU'LL NEED TO PITCH YOURSELF TO RADIO

Alex Carroll has seven things prepared ahead of time when he attempts to book himself on radio shows. If that's your goal, too, you should also have these things in place.

1. A good show idea, a good topic, or a good hook.

"Remember you're selling a show to the station, not a product," says Alex. "They know you're selling a product, but to the radio or TV people, you're selling them a show—that's what they're interested in."

2. A toll-free number.

"I have a toll-free number, and I also have a Web site," notes Alex. "Toll-free numbers aren't as important as they used to be. Your Web site is more important on the radio now, but you should still have a toll-free number."

3. The ability to accept credit cards.

"That's pretty much a no-brainer," Alex comments.

4. Credentials.

"There are two kinds of credentials," observes Alex. "There are degrees, job titles, awards, foundations and organizations, all those letters behind your name. That's one kind. But it's not the best kind. The other kind of credential is called 'experiential credentials,' and it's better. I have experiential credentials. I'm an ex-courier driver. I actually beat eight out of ten speeding tickets."

5. A good, clear phone line.

"Most of your interviews will be by telephone," Alex says. "You need to know how to disable your call waiting. Having a call-recorder is a really good idea because then you can listen to your interviews afterwards and go back and critique yourself."

6. A current data base of all the top radio shows.

"I have one available at www.RadioPublicity.com," Alex reports.

7. A press kit.

"You need to have both a physical press kit and an online press kit," Alex advises. "Some people say, 'I just want to have a Web site and put my press releases up and send people there.' That's not good enough. If you actually take the time to put together a nice press kit and send it to them, you've made a wise investment. It's a lot more difficult for them to just blow you off. Why? Guilt."

JM: Who do you contact to get on radio shows?

AC: You call the producers. The hosts usually don't book guests—the producers do. Smaller markets don't have producers because they can't afford them. You'll know when you call that if the host books the guest, it's a small station.

When calling a producer of a show, know that they stick around for an hour and a half after their show and then they go home. Don't call before the show; call after the show. Before the show, they're prepping. They're really busy getting ready to start the show.

JM: How should you pitch a producer once you get him or her on the phone?

AC: Build a relationship. That's what it boils down to. You have to keep your pitch short. When I get a producer on the phone or I get their voice mail, I simply say,"My name is Alex Carroll and I wrote a book on how to beat speeding tickets and I thought with the... (pick your holiday, Fourth of July, Memorial Day, Christmas)...coming up and all the speed traps that are going to be out, I thought you guys might be interested in having me as a guest on your show so I can help all of your listeners who got nailed over the weekend or who will get nailed in the upcoming weekend. If you're interested, I'd be happy to send you a copy of my book and a press kit. Here's my phone number, call me back." That's it! It's like fifteen or twenty seconds and I'm done. You have to get to the point quickly.

When you call a producer the first time, 95 percent of the time you're going to get their voice mail. Leave them a message just like I said, a short pitch. Then two days later, call them back. Don't expect them to call you back; it's up to you to follow up.

Two days later you follow up and you get their voice mail again, most likely. You hit "0" (zero) this time and it takes you back to the operator. When the operator picks up, you say, "Hey I got Joe's voice mail. Is there any chance you can page him for me?" It's that simple. If they're not in the studio or stuck somewhere else, they'll usually pick up the phone and talk to you.

You're probably thinking, "Dude, you have some serious *cajones* to page these guys at work. What are you thinking?" Here's the thing— you have to shift your mode of thinking from one of begging, "Please book me on your show," to serving. "Hey, I have a really great show for you guys. You're going to love this. It's perfect for you." That's it! Go from begging to serving. It's that simple.

JM: Are live or taped interviews better?

AC: You always want to do a live interview. Time slots are so important. If you do a taped interview, you have absolutely no control over when that interview will air. You don't even know if it *will* air. They may edit out your contact information, your Web site, or your toll-free number. You want to do a live interview.

JM: What about the interview itself?

AC: The first thing to know is you have to take charge of your interview. Most guests are passive when they go on a show. They're waiting for the hosts to interview them and ask them questions. Not me. When I get on a show, I'm aggressive. I have an agenda. I have seven to ten bullet points that I want to get out while I'm on that show because I know the more information I can get out during the interview, the more people are going to want to buy my book. It's just the way it is. The more you give, the more you get. So you want to take charge of your interview.

In the first 60 seconds, you have to capture the audience and make sure they don't go anyplace else. After you've done that, then you want to launch right into your agenda, which are your seven to ten bullet points. You have to entertain and enlighten the audience. You want to accomplish those two things when you're doing your interview.

JM: How do you get your plug in?

AC: When you come to the close. That is your plug. The barter arrangement is you did a good show and as long as you did a good show, you get your plug. Never leave without your plug.

JM: What's the best way to get invited back?

AC: Always send a thank you letter after you do an interview and your thank you letter should go something like this: "Thanks so much for the opportunity to be on your show this morning (afternoon/evening). I look forward to returning and being on your show again in the future."

Notice that you're already planting the seed that you want to be a guest again. Then you also want to say, "By the way, if you ever have a guest cancel on you at the last minute and you need somebody in a pinch, feel free to call me. Here's my cell phone number." That's a nice gesture; they really appreciate it, and sometimes they do call you. I've had it happen to me several times.

JM: Any other words of advice?

AC: This whole media thing is about relentless persistence and coming at it with the mindset and attitude that's not "if" I get on the show, it's "when." That's my attitude, and that's all you have to do. I'm tenacious, but I'm also totally polite.

If I get to a point where I've called the producer a bunch of times, I'll just say, "Hey, am I bugging you?" Every once in a while, they'll say, "Yes, you're bugging me," and I'll reply, "OK, cool, I'll go away for a while and I'll come back in a year." But usually they'll just say, "Nah, you're not bugging me. Actually at some point in time, we're going to do your topic. So if you keep calling me, sooner or later we'll book you."

When you're on a program, be sure to ask the producer if you can have a copy of the interview. When you have some recordings you're proud of, you'll have samples you can send to radio producers who request them. Better yet, make clips available on the media center of your Web site, and direct the producers there. Get permission to post them first, though.

CHAPTER 17

Becoming an Internet Celebrity

"Tie a famous name to your product. It doesn't matter if they are a celebrity, a celebrity impersonator, or just named after a celebrity... the press loves using celebrity names."

Trafficology.com

The Internet has recently undergone a transformation that makes it incredibly easy—and pretty much free—for you to promote yourself and your business online. This transformation is widely known as "Web 2.0." What it really means is the sudden evolution of the Web from static to more dynamic and user-generated content.

The Web (as we knew it from 1993 to about 2001) was mostly made up of Web pages that didn't change unless the Webmaster made them. Web 2.0 (which began around 2001) means users are now creating most of the content. Sites such as Wikipedia (www.Wikipedia.com), Facebook (www.Facebook.com), LinkedIn (www.LinkedIn.com), Squidoo (www.Squidoo.com), Twitter (www.Twitter.com), YouTube (www.YouTube.com), and blogs allow the visitor to easily create, publish, and comment on content that others can see. This gives you an enormous advantage if you want to create a personal brand on the Web and an online presence for your business, product or service.

Below are some of the most popular ways to get started using Web 2.0. But don't fear—although the term may sound a bit technical, Web 2.0 is actually very simple and easy to put into action. That's actually one of the best aspects of Web 2.0 vs. Web 1.0—no programming skills are required, it's much easier to use, and anyone can do it.

SQUIDOO

Founded by marketing expert and author Seth Godin (www.SethGodin.com), Squidoo (www.Squidoo.com) is, according to its Web site, "the world's most popular site for people who want to build a page about their passions." It's fast and free to start a "lens," which Squidoo calls "one person's view on a topic that matters to him." It's an easy-to-build single Web page that can point to blogs, favorite links, RSS feeds, Flickr photos, Google maps, your eBay auctions, CafePress designs, Amazon books or music, and more. When someone is looking for recommended information fast, your lens gets him started and sends him in the right direction.

Visit Squidoo.com to download Seth Godin's free e-book, *Everyone Is an Expert... About Something,* to help you get started.

YOUTUBE

Creating a YouTube (www.YouTube.com) video is a great way to get booked on TV talk shows.

Consider this: Most TV show Web sites feature a "Be on the Show" section with topics that producers are actively working on, along with how to contact them online. Instead of just sending the producer an e-mail pitch, you can include a link to your most relevant YouTube video.

That accomplishes two important things. One, it shows that you're media savvy. Two, it allows the producer to see your face and how you'll "appear" on television. One of my clients created a YouTube video on a topic that producers were looking for at the *Oprah* Web site (www.Oprah.com), and included a link to her video in her e-mail to the producer. The producer contacted her within a few days.

But don't send your YouTube video link only to producers. Use it on your Web site or blog, as well. You can also create multiple videos for a YouTube "channel," a collection of your videos to which visitors can subscribe. They'll get automatic updates when you upload new ones.

YouTube is also a great way to get publicity for yourself and your products, because its video search results now appear on Google. A short video I posted of me with nightlife impresario Amanda Lepore has been viewed numerous times, though I haven't promoted it at all. Imagine what you can do with a little effort.

BECOME A CELEBRITY BLOGGER

Blogs are short for "web logs." Think of them as an online journal or diary for your business. Bloggers write and publish entries (called "posts") on their blogs daily, weekly or at random. Some of the most popular bloggers post several times a day. Many people still think of blogs as stream-of-consciousness ramblings about what the blogger did that day, what they ate for lunch, and other life trivialities. But you don't have to use them like that. If you own a business, you should have a blog.

A blog serves three main purposes for business owners. First, it gains customer loyalty because you can share thoughts with your customers about how and why your company operates, either through posts from you or your employees. Second, it helps your company's Web site get ranked higher up in search engines, because major ones such as Google prefer sites that have constantly updated content. Third, blogs create community and involvement because they allow readers to add comments to posts.

So while you can still have your "brochure" Web site that doesn't charge much, you or your webmaster can easily add a blog. It's best to update your blog daily. If you can't do that, weekly is OK. But if you can't update your blog at least once a week, it's probably not worth your time or money setting one up.

So what do you write about on your blog? On my blog CELEBRITY | PR (www.CELEBRITYPR.com), I post news and updates about my business and my clients. Blog posts should be short and sweet, because reading text on a computer screen is much harder on the eyes than reading text on paper. You also want your posts to be easy for the reader to scan. If they have to read pages and pages of thoughts, they'll just get annoyed and click to another Web site.

Success Story: Perez Hilton, PerezHilton.com

Mario Armando Lavandeira Jr. started blogging and gossiping about celebrities because, as he says, "it seemed easy." His blog, Perez Hilton (www.PerezHilton.com), soon caught on with readers. Currently, more than two million people view it every day (and up to seven million when he breaks a major celebrity story). Lavandeira has since taken the name of his blog, calling himself Perez Hilton. When Britney Spears shaved her head, Hilton saw more than 4.75 million unique visitors to his site in a 24-hour period. All this exposure has led to his guest appearances on Donald Trump's *The Apprentice*, Kathy Griffin's *My Life on the D-List*, the *Janice Dickinson Modeling Agency*, MTV's *Celebrity Rap Superstar*, and E!'s *Keeping Up with the Kardashians*. He's cohosted *The View* and had his own reality show on VH1 called *What Perez Sez*!

In Hilton's case, his blog is his business. So every appearance he does on television or in magazines like *Vanity Fair* and newspapers like the *Los Angeles Times* is great Celebrity Leverage. But you don't have to be Perez Hilton to become a celebrity by having your own blog.

If you don't want to maintain your own blog, you should at least leverage the power of other blogs and bloggers. Timothy Ferriss (www.TimothyFerriss.com), the young entrepreneur who wrote the instant *New York Times* best-seller *The 4-Hour Workweek* (www.4HourWorkweek.com), credits much of his book's success to getting it mentioned on other well-known blogs.

The business blogging solution I prefer is TypePad (www.TypePad.com). It's a hosted service (although you can use your own domain name) that has two important benefits: It's continually updated with new features, and it's extremely easy to use. TypePad costs $149 per year, which comes out to only about $12 per month. That's about the cost of a regular Web host, yet it rivals most industry-standard Web hosting plans. TypePad also has a section on its site that features interesting business blogs, so if yours is really good, TypePad may even help promote it.

If you're looking for a free solution, WordPress (www.WordPress.org) is popular open-source (meaning free) software. It's probably the most popular blogging software available, but it's also a bit more technically challenging to use than TypePad (although more customizable). You'll have to install some updates and fix bugs yourself, so as a busy business person (unless you're paying someone to run your blog for you), you might prefer to use a hosted service.

After blogging for a year or more, you may find you have enough posts to turn them into a book. After writing the best-selling marketing books *Purple Cow, Free Prize Inside!* and *Unleashing the Idea Virus*, Seth Godin (www.SethGodin.com) decided to turn his blog into a book. Soon after, *Small Is the New Big: and 183 Other Riffs, Rants, and Remarkable Business Ideas* was born. It's simply a collection of Godin's best blog posts. Services such as Blurb (www.Blurb.com) will even pull your posts and create a book for you. How easy is that?

Insider Interview: Brian Reich, Cone Inc.

Brian Reich, director of new media for Cone Inc. (www.ConeInc. com), a strategy and media communications agency in Boston, has worked with many business and nonprofit clients helping them better compete using today's various online social media tools. He is the coauthor of *Media Rules! Mastering Today's Technology to Connect With and Keep Your Audience* and the blog *Thinking About Media* (www.ThinkingAboutMedia.com).

I spoke with Brian about how you can use the new power of Web 2.0 to make your business a star

JORDAN MCAULEY: How important are blogs to help promote a new product or existing business?

BR: At last check, the blog tracking service Technorati (www.Technorati.com) was tracking between 700,000 and five million blogs worldwide. More than 120,000 blogs are created every day. There are individual blogs, community blogs, photo blogs, and blogs that are only updated by mobile phone. The range of topics, depth and expertise now available is staggering.

Organizations can easily launch blogs, but their success will depend on how they use them. Just the same, organizations can look to engage the blogosphere in the hopes that they'll help carry a key message or provide an endorsement that moves its way across the Web. Either way, the audience for blogs, particularly customers who are looking to understand details about a new product, or media who are looking for angles to cover a new venture, want information that goes beyond traditional marketing speak or advertising jargon. They respond to honesty and transparent communications, passionate views, and biting opinions.

Organizations should not launch a blog simply to make content more available or to reach out to bloggers simply to prove that they can. Like any other communications opportunity, organizations must look at wading into the blogosphere as an opportunity to add something interesting, relevant or timely to the discussion. And if they can't, then there are plenty of other ways to add your voice that may be more appropriate.

JM: What are the most effective ways for charities to take advantage of new media?

BR: There are dozens of major nonprofit groups and advocacy organizations who have mobilized their audiences to action, raised millions of dollars through small donations, and captured the attention of media, government and world powers as a result of their actions online. Look at the campaigns waged by the ONE Campaign, MoveOn, St. Jude Children's Research Hospital, DonorsChoose, and the Susan G. Komen Breast Cancer Foundation — they have demonstrated an understanding of how the Internet complements their other efforts and generated success on a variety of levels. These groups have expanded their reach and impact into our society through their online campaigns, and they raise the bar for everyone in the process. Sadly, they are more often the exception than the rule.

JM: Can a small business flourish without using blogs, e-mail, etc.? Can a company grow with just a bare-bones Web site?

BR: Online, you have to do more than just post some information, a logo, or send an e-mail to show your commitment. Users expect to immerse themselves in an issue. They want to have some choice in what the organizations they support do and how they invest both their time and dollars. They want to see that their efforts are having a real, measurable impact. The same tenets of good marketing and communication apply to charitable organizations and nonprofit groups, online or off, no matter the issue, no matter the cause.

Too often, the decisions that organizations make when it comes to online marketing are dictated by the "shiny object syndrome," a terrible affliction that results in a marketing path based on whatever is newest or generating the most buzz at the moment, instead of what will truly be effective.

For example, when a company learns that more than 60 million people use MySpace, they say, "Wonderful! We'll launch a MySpace profile." Or when an executive hears about the size of the blogosphere (75 million and growing), she demands, "We must do that, too." These decisions are often made without consideration for what the audience will respond to, and what will help meet the organization's communications goals.

Organizations must find a new and different technique to reach and engage people effectively around a product launch, important issue, or announcement of key information. The expectations people now have about how, and what, information will be available to them continue to grow and change. As consumers are given more choices about what to buy, who to read, and how to communicate with each other, we can help. When successfully merged with a focused communications strategy, a new media strategy can help an organization communicate more directly and effectively — and therefore distinguish itself as a strategic leader.

DON'T GET OVERWHELMED!

Thinking about your strategy for using Web 2.0 can feel overwhelming at first. With earlier Web 1.0 static Web pages, businesses often used the same marketing strategies online as they did in the offline world. Now, however, they have to think differently about how to communicate. Decide which of the new Web 2.0 social media tools makes the most sense for your target market, and jump in!

Afterword

TIME TO USE YOUR NEW STAR POWER

Now you're armed with all the information you need to add powerful Celebrity Leverage to your business, either by affiliating yourself with celebrities or elevating yourself, your business or your product to celebrity status.

Not only do you have the knowledge but you also have some awesome resources and partners who will help you on your journey to greater visibility. Be persistent, and you'll begin to see how Celebrity Leverage can make all the difference.

I look forward to hearing your success stories. Please send them to me at jordan@contactanycelebrity.com.

Reach for the stars,

Jordan McAuley
CELEBRITY | PR

P.S. Now that you've learned the basics of Celebrity Leverage, check out www.CelebrityLeverage.com to discover advanced secrets from even more experts.

See you at www.CelebrityLeverage.com!

Bonus Chapter

Rhonda Rees, former president of the Los Angeles Publicity Club and author of *Profit & Prosper with Public Relations*, offers these additional tips for getting media coverage:

1. Consider using a press clipping service to obtain any print and online media coverage received that you may not know about. Alternatively, you can run an online search on Google News (news.google.com) for free.

2. When sending a pitch letter to radio and television producers, it's a good idea to rubber-stamp the document with "Interview Guest Available" in red ink near the top of the page. This way the booking contact can tell right away what you have in mind before reading through—or tossing out—your information.

3. If you're an author, keep in mind cable television's Book TV (www.BookTV.org) on C-SPAN2, as it offers 48 hours of continuous nonfiction book programming every weekend.

4. When pitching electronic media, let radio and television stations know when you'll be near their studios. This might help you land an interview if the media understand that you only have a limited amount of time for an appearance.

5. It's always a good idea to hold your special event at a location close to a freeway and not too far from radio and TV stations. A convenient site location increases the odds that the media will want to cover your event.

6. Should you land an interview, it's important to note that by the time of its airing, your company name may be omitted by the station's editing. Solutions include carefully mentioning your company or product name while answering a question, wearing a

T-shirt with a logo or other identifier, or placing a company banner in the background. Use subtlety; you don't want to overdo it.

7. When pitching feature stories, it's a smart idea to review newspaper and magazine editorial calendars in advance, so you'll know what subjects these publications are interested in covering throughout the year. Contact their advertising departments and ask for a press kit, or subscribe to online editorial calendar services such as EdCals (www.MyEdCals.com).

8. If you want to pitch an innovative, high-tech story to the media, contact the CyberGuy (www.CyberGuy.com), otherwise known as Kurt Knutsson. He's the leading journalist covering Internet topics, with a nationally syndicated computer and technology report online and on radio and television stations. Kurt's programs air three to five times a week in several American cities, reaching an audience of 48 million people.

9. To help guide PR people through the never-ending maze of newer media and technologies, Bulldog Reporter (www.BulldogReporter.com) recently published the handbook *Revolution in PR Technology: PR Practitioner's Field Guide to New Media Solutions*.

10. When you secure that all-important media coverage and the public calls for more information on your product or service, make sure your staff is prepared to handle those requests along with follow-up materials. Have your staff ask callers where they saw or heard about your company so you can track the media source.

Celebrity Leverage Experts

Susan Berkley
The Great Voice Company, Inc.

www.GreatVoice.com

Alex Carroll
Radio Publicty

www.RadioPublicity.com

Jeff Crilley
Real News Public Relations

www.RealNewsPR.com

Donna Cutting
Donna Cutting Presents

www.DonnaCutting.com

Mike Esterman
Esterman Entertainment

www.Esterman.com

Brian Patrick Flynn
www.BrianPatrickFlynn.com

Rick Frishman
Planned Television Arts

www.RickFrishman.com

Drew Gerber
Wasabi Publicity, Inc.

www.MyPressKit247.com

www.WasabiPublicity.com

Jake Halpern
www.JakeHalpern.com

Bill & Steve Harrison
Bradley Communications

www.RTIR.com

www.PublicitySummit.com

Susan Harrow
PR Secrets

www.AppearOnOprah.com

www.6FigureBookAdvance.com

Paul Hartunian
Free Publicity Information Center

www.Hartunian.com

Craig Hirschfeld
How to Hire A Celebrity

www.HowToHireACelebrity.com

Dan Janal
PR Leads

www.Janal.com

www.MyPRLeads.com

Gavin Keilly
GBK Productions

www.GBKProductions.com

Dan Kennedy
Glazer-Kennedy Inner Circle, Inc.

www.DanKennedyPresents.com

John Kremer
Open Horizons

www.BookMarket.com

Rebecca Lightsey
Gifted Presence

www.GiftedPresence.net

Ann McIndoo
www.AnnMcIndoo.com

www.SoYouWantToWrite.com

Rhonda Rees
Former President

Los Angeles Publicity Club

Brian Reich
Thinking About Media

www.ThinkingAboutMedia.com

Nick Romer
Sell on Q

www.SellOnQ.com

Penny Sansevieri
Author Marketing Experts, Inc.

www.AMarketingExpert.com

Yanik Silver
Surefire Marketing, Inc.

www.SurefireMarketing.com

www.MaverickBusinessAdventures.com

Robyn Spizman
www.RobynSpizman.com

www.SpizmanAgency.com

Joan Stewart
The Publicity Hound

www.PublicityHound.com

Amy Stumpf
Gift List Media

www.MyGiftListMedia.com

www.MySpotlightBranding.com

Joe Vitale
www.MrFire.com

www.MyHypnoticMarketing.com

Anthony Zelig
New York Celebrity Assistants Association

www.NYCelebrityAssistants.org

RECOMMENDED RESOURCES:

BLOGGING SOFTWARE

Blogger
www.Blogger.com

TypePad
www.TypePad.com

WordPress
www.WordPress.org

BOOKS

*The Celebrity Black Book: Over 55,000
Accurate Celebrity Addresses*
Jordan McAuley

*Celebrity Branding You: A Revolutionary System for Entre-
preneurs and Professionals to Become the Go-To Expert,
Dominate Your Field and Eliminate the Competition*
J.W. Dicks & Nick Nanton

*The Celebrity Experience: Insider Secrets to Deliv-
ering Red Carpet Customer Service*
Donna Cutting

Celebrity Sells
Hamish Pringle

*Fame Junkies: The Hidden Truths Behind
America's Favorite Addiction*
Jake Halpern

*Get Slightly Famous: Become a Celebrity in Your Field
and Attract More Business with Less Effort*
Steven Van Yoder

*High Visibility: Transforming Your Personal
and Professional Brand*
Irving Rein

*The Importance of Being Famous: Behind the
Scenes of the Celebrity-Industrial Complex*
Maureen Orth

*No B.S. Marketing to the Affluent: The No Holds Barred,
Kick Butt, Take No Prisoners Guide to Getting Really Rich*
Dan Kennedy

*Red Carpet Suicide: A Survival Guide on
Keeping Up with the Hiltons*
Perez Hilton

*Secrets to Contacting Celebrities and Public Figures:
101 Ways to Reach the Rich & Famous*
Jordan McAuley

Speak to Influence: How to Unlock the Hidden Power of Your Voice
Susan Berkley

*Starring You!: The Insider's Guide to Using Television and
Media to Launch Your Brand, Your Business, and Your Life*
Marta Tracy & Terence Noonan with Karen Kelly

*There's a Customer Born Every Minute: P.T. Barnum's
Amazing 10 "Rings of Power" for Creating Fame, Fortune,
and a Business Empire Today—Guaranteed!*
Joe Vitale and Jeffrey Gitomer

*Where's My Fifteen Minutes?: Get Your Company, Your
Cause, or Yourself the Recognition You Deserve*
Howard Bragman

CELEBRITY APPEARANCE BOOKERS

Mike Esterman
Esterman Entertainment
www.Esterman.com

Craig Hirschfeld
How to Hire a Celebrity
www.HowToHireACelebrity.com

Jack King
Celeb Brokers
www.CelebBrokers.com

Rita Tateel
Celebrity Source
www.CelebritySource.com

CELEBRITY CONTACT INFORMATION

Celebrity Addresses Online
www.CelebrityAddresses.com

Contact Any Celebrity
www.ContactAnyCelebrity.com

Screen Actors Guild (SAG)
www.SAG.org

Actors to Locate Link: 323-549-6737

Secrets to Contacting Celebrities
www.SecretsToContactingCelebrities.com

CELEBRITY FUND-RAISING

Celebrity Causes Database
www.CelebCauses.com

Celebrity Fundraising
www.CelebrityFundraising.com

Help from Hollywood
www.HelpFromHollywood.com

CELEBRITY GIFT BAGS

Karen Wood
Backstage Creations
www.BackstageCreations.com

Rebecca Lightsey
Gifted Presence
www.GiftedPresence.net

Julie Kenney
Jewels and Pinstripes
www.JewelsAndPinstripes.com

Melissa Lerner
The Silver Spoon
www.TheSilverSpoon.com

CELEBRITY GIFT BASKETS

Phyllis Pometta
Baby Swags
www.BabySwags.com

CELEBRITY GIFT SUITES

Karen Wood
Backstage Creations
www.BackstageCreations.com

Gavin Keilly
GBK Productions
www.GBKProductions.com

CELEBRITY PHOTOS

Mr. Paparazzi
www.MrPaparazzi.com

Perez Hilton
www.PerezHilton.com

PR Photos
www.PRPhotos.com

Scoopt
www.Scoopt.com

TMZ
www.TMZ.com

WireImage
www.WireImage.com

X17 Online
www.X17Online.com

CELEBRITY SPEAKERS

National Speakers Association
www.NSASpeaker.org

Big Speak
www.BigSpeak.com

Greater Talent Network
www.GreaterTalent.com

IMG Speakers
www.IMGSpeakers.com

Leigh Bureau
www.LeighBureau.com

Premiere Speakers
www.PremiereSpeakers.com

Speakers Platform
www.Speaking.com

Total Access Speakers
www.TotalAccessSpeakers.com

Washington Speakers Bureau
www.WashingtonSpeakers.com

CELEBRITY VOICES

Susan Berkley
The Great Voice Company
www.GreatVoice.com

VoiceShot
www.VoiceShot.com

Voice 123
www.Voice123.com

Voice Recruiters
www.VoiceRecruiters.com

Voices.com
www.Voices.com

CELEBRITY WRANGLERS

Capian Enterprises
www.CapianEnterprises.com

Celebrity Source
www.CelebritySource.com

Fingerprint Communications
www.FingerprintCom.net

Flying Television
www.FlyingTelevision.com

Full Picture PR
www.FullPic.com

Xenii
www.Xenii.com

E-MAIL SERVICES

AWeber
www.AWeber.com

Constant Contact
www.ConstantContact.com

iContact
www.iContact.com

GetResponse
www.MyGetResponse.com

EVENT LOCATIONS

Paramount Pictures
www.Paramount.com

Playboy Mansion
www.PartyWithTheBunnies.com

NBC Universal Studios
www.nbcuni.com/studio

Roundabout Theatre Company (Studio 54)
www.RoundaboutTheatre.org

Warner Bros. Studio
www.WBSpecialEvents.com

GIFT GUIDES

Amy Stumpf
Gift List Media
www.MyGiftListMedia.com

MARKETING AND PUBLICITY

American Marketing Association
www.MarketingPower.com

Bulldog Reporter
www.BulldogReporter.com

Celebrity Branding You
www.CelebrityBrandingYou.com

Celebrity Leverage
www.CelebrityLeverage.com

Get Booked on Oprah
www.AppearOnOprah.com

National Publicity Summit
www.PublicitySummit.com

Partyline
www.PartylinePublishing.com

Paul Hartunian
www.Hartunian.com

Planned Television Arts
www.PlannedTVArts.com

PQ Media
www.PQMedia.com

PR Leads
www.MyPRLeads.com

PR Secrets
www.MyPRSecrets.com

Press Kit 24/7
www.MyPressKit247.com

Publicity Hound
www.PublicityHound.com

Publicity Insider
www.PublicityInsider.com

Radio-TV Interview Report (RTIR)
www.RTIR.com

PRODUCT PLACEMENT

Amy Stumpf
Spotlight Branding
www.MySpotlightBranding.com

Backstage Creations
www.BackstageCreations.com

Distinctive Assets
www.DistinctiveAssets.com

Game Show Placements
www.GameShowPlacements.com

On 3 Productions
www.On3Productions.com

Product Placement International
www.ProductPlacementInternational.com

Rogers & Cowan
www.RogersAndCowan.com

PUBLISHING AND WRITING

Adam Witty
Advantage Media
www.advantagefamily.com

Rick Frishman
Author 101
www.Author101.com

Blurb
www.Blurb.com

CreateSpace
www.CreateSpace.com

Get a 6 Figure Book Advance
www.6FigureBookAdvance.com

Independent Book Publishers Association (IBPA)
www.PMA-Online.org

Lightning Source
www.LightningSource.com

Lulu
www.Lulu.com

Make Your Book Famous
www.MakeYourBookFAmous.com

Para Publishing
www.ParaPublishing.com

Paul Hartunian
Book Market
www.BookMarket.com

Small Publishers Association of North America (SPAN)
www.SpanNet.org

RADIO PUBLICITY

Radio Publicity
www.RadioPublicity.com

Radio-TV Interview Report
www.RTIR.com

REALITY TV

Reality TV Casting Call
www.RealityTVCastingCall.com

Reality TV Web Site
www.RealityTVWebSite.com

Reality Wanted
www.RealityWanted.com

SOCIAL NETWORKS

Facebook
www.Facebook.com

LinkedIn
www.LinkedIn.com

MySpace
www.MySpace.com

TELEVISION PUBLICITY

Guide to Top National TV Talk & Interview Shows
www.AppearOnTopTVShows.com

Planned Television Arts
www.PlannedTVArts.com

Radio-TV Interview Report
www.RTIR.com

TOOLS FOR EVALUATING CELEBRITY APPEAL

Forbes Celebrity 100
www.forbes.com/celebrity100

Google Fight
www.GoogleFight.com

Nielsen Media Research
www.NielsenMedia.com

Survey Monkey
www.SurveyMonkey.com

Q Scores
www.QScores.com

Web Poll
webpoll.sparklit.com

TRADE PUBLICATIONS

Backstage
www.Backstage.com

Billboard
www.Billboard.com

The Hollywood Reporter
www.HollywoodReporter.com

Variety
www.Variety.com

WEB 2.0

Squidoo
www.Squidoo.com

Twitter
www.Twitter.com

YouTube
www.YouTube.com

Glossary

Agent - (see "Talent Agent")

Blog - (short for "web log") is a Web site that provides commentary or news on a particular subject or that functions as an online diary. A typical blog includes entries in reverse chronological order and combines text, images, and links to other blogs, Web pages, and other media related to its topic. The ability for readers to leave comments in an interactive format is an important part of many blogs. Most blogs are primarily textual, although some focus on art (artlog), photographs (photoblog), sketches (sketchblog), videos (vlog), music (MP3blog), and audio (podcasting). "Blog" can also be used as a verb, meaning to maintain or add content to a blog.

Celebrity - A widely recognized or famous person who commands a high degree of public and media attention. The word stems from the Latin verb "celebre" meaning famous, renowned. Mass entertainment personalities such as actors or music stars are likely to become celebrities even if the person deliberately avoids media attention.

Endorsement - A written or spoken statement from a public figure or a private citizen, extolling the virtue of some product. The term "testimonial" most commonly applies to the sales pitches attributed to ordinary citizens, whereas "endorsement" usually applies to sales pitches by celebrities.

Manager - (see "Talent Manager")

Paparazzi - A plural term for photographers who take candid photographs of celebrities, usually by relentlessly shadowing them in their public and private activities. The word "paparazzi" was popularized after the Federico Fellini 1960 film *La Dolce Vita*. One of the characters is a news photographer named Paparazzo (played by Walter Santesso).

Product Placement - Promotional ads placed by marketers using real commercial products and services in media, where the presence of a particular brand is the result of an economic exchange. Product placement appears in plays, film, television series, music videos, video games and books. It became more common starting in the 1980s but can be traced back to at least 1949. Product placement puts the brand's logo in a shot, or makes a favorable mention or appearance of a product in a shot. This is done without disclosure and under the pretext that it's a natural part of the work.

Publicist - A person whose job is to generate and manage publicity for a public figure, especially for a celebrity, or for a work such as a book or film. Publicists usually work at large companies handling multiple clients. In the world of celebrities, publicists typically take a flat monthly fee for service to a client, whereas agents and managers tend to take a percentage of their client's gross income.

Swag - (Short for "Samples, Wearables and Gifts") usually refers to promotional items or gifts that are given away by companies or organizations often at trade shows, conferences, festivals or gala events. Companies that provide expensive gifts for celebrity attendees often ask that the celebrities allow a photo to be taken of them with the gift item, which can be used by the company for promotional purposes. Other companies provide luxury gifts such as handbags or scarves to celebrity attendees in the hopes that the celebrities will wear these items in public, thus garnering publicity for the company's brand name and product.

Talent Agent - A person who finds jobs for actors, musicians, models, and other people in various entertainment businesses. Agents make their money by taking a percentage of the money that their client is paid. Different regulations govern various types of agents; the regulations are established by artists' unions and the legal jurisdiction in which the agent operates. (Also see "Talent Manager.")

Talent Manager - Also known as a personal manager, a talent manager is a person or company guiding the professional care of artists in the entertainment industry. The talent manager oversees the day-to-day business affairs of the artist, and advises on professional matters, long-term plans and personal decisions that may affect the artist's career. The roles and responsibilities of a talent manager vary slightly from industry to industry, as do the commissions to which the manager is entitled. For example, the duties of a music manager differ from those who advise actors, writers or directors. A manager can also help artists find an agent, or help them decide when to fire their current agent and identify a new one. Talent agents have the authority to make deals for their clients, while managers usually can only informally establish connections with products and studios but do not have the authority to negotiate contracts.

Web 2.0 - Refers to a perceived second generation of Web-based communities and hosted services—such as social networking sites and wikis—that aim to facilitate collaboration and sharing among users. The term became popular following the first O'Reilly Media Web 2.0 conference in 2004 and has since become widely adapted.

About the Author

Jordan McAuley is founder and president of CELEBRITY | PR (www.CELEBRITYPR.com), a media and public relations firm in New York City that specializes in strategic marketing and publicity. Known as the "King of Celebrity Contacts," he has more than a decade's experience in publicity, marketing, publishing, events and entrepreneurship.

His Contact Any Celebrity (www.ContactAnyCelebrity.com) service is one of the most respected publicity resources in the world, with billings of more than $1 million annually and a blue-chip roster of more than 5,000 marketers, publicists, nonprofits, journalists and media clients who rely on it daily.

McAuley and his clients have been featured by the *Associated Press*, *USA Today*, *Wall Street Journal*, *Investor's Business Daily*, *Star Magazine*, *Village Voice*, *Entrepreneur Magazine*, *Out Magazine*, *New York Magazine*, and others. He has also appeared on CNN, National Public Radio (NPR), E! Online, Q Television, Better TV, and Sirius/XM Satellite Radio.

He got his start as an intern in the publicity departments of CNN and Turner Entertainment in Atlanta. He also worked at a prominent modeling agency in South Beach, Miami; a film production company in Hollywood, California; and a top talent agency in Beverly Hills.

McAuley is featured in several best-selling books including Timothy Ferris' *The 4-Hour Workweek*, Dan Kennedy's *Marketing to the Affluent*, Dan Poynter's *Publishing Encyclopedia*, John Kremer's *1001 Ways to Market Your Books*, Robin Blakely's *Get PR Therapy*, and Tsufit's *Step Into the Spotlight: A Guide to Getting Noticed*.

He is the author of the best-selling *Celebrity Black Book* and *Secrets to Contacting Celebrities and Public Figures: 101 Ways to Reach the Rich and Famous.* He also coauthored *Secrets of Peak Performers* with Dan Kennedy, Bill Glazer and Lee Milteer.

He is a member of the Public Relations Society of America (PRSA), the Independent Book Publishers Association (IBPA), the Information Marketing Association (IMA), the GLAAD Media Circle, and the Association of Fundraising Professionals (AFP).

McAuley was born and raised in Atlanta, Georgia. He graduated with a bachelor of science in communication (motion picture business and English literature) from the University of Miami in 2000. He resides in New York City where he enjoys power yoga and fancy cupcakes.

Visit Contact Any Celebrity (www.ContactAnyCelebrity.com) to search his online Rolodex, and CELEBRITY | PR at www.CELEBRITYPR.com for his blog, tools and resources.

www.CELEBRITYPR.com
www.ContactAnyCelebrity.com

FEDERAL TRADE COMMISSION 16 CFR Part 255

Guides Concerning the Use of Endorsements and Testimonials in Advertising

* * * *

This document includes only the text of the Revised Endorsement and Testimonial Guides. To learn more, read the Federal Register Notice at **www.ftc.gov/opa/2009/10/endortest.shtm.**

* * * *

§ 255.0   Purpose and definitions.

(a) The Guides in this part represent administrative interpretations of laws enforced by the Federal Trade Commission for the guidance of the public in conducting its affairs in conformity with legal requirements. Specifically, the Guides address the application of Section 5 of the FTC Act (15 U.S.C. 45) to the use of endorsements and testimonials in advertising. The Guides provide the basis for voluntary compliance with the law by advertisers and endorsers. Practices inconsistent with these Guides may result in corrective action by the Commission under Section 5 if, after investigation, the Commission has reason to believe that the practices fall within the scope of conduct declared unlawful by the statute. The Guides set forth the general principles that the Commission will use in evaluating endorsements and testimonials, together with examples illustrating the application of those principles. The Guides do not purport to cover every possible use of endorsements in advertising. Whether a particular endorsement or testimonial is deceptive will depend on the specific factual circumstances of the advertisement at issue.

(b) For purposes of this part, an endorsement means any advertising message (including verbal statements, demonstrations, or depictions of the name, signature, likeness or other identifying personal characteristics of an individual or the name or seal of an organization) that consumers are likely to believe reflects the opinions, beliefs, findings, or experiences of a party other than the sponsoring advertiser, even if the views expressed by that party are identical to those of the sponsoring advertiser. The party whose opinions, beliefs, findings, or experience the message appears to reflect will be called the endorser and may be an individual, group, or institution.

(c) The Commission intends to treat endorsements and testimonials identically in the context of its enforcement of the Federal Trade Commission Act and for purposes of this part. The term endorsements is therefore generally used hereinafter to cover both terms and situations.

(d) For purposes of this part, the term product includes any product, service, company or industry.

(e) For purposes of this part, an expert is an individual, group, or institution possessing, as a result of experience, study, or training, knowledge of a particular subject, which knowledge is superior to what ordinary individuals generally acquire.

Example 1: A film critic's review of a movie is excerpted in an advertisement. When so used, the review meets the definition of an endorsement because it is viewed by readers as a statement of the critic's own opinions and not those of the film producer, distributor, or exhibitor. Any alteration in or quotation from the text of the review that does not fairly reflect its substance would be a violation of the standards set by this part because it would distort the endorser's opinion. [See § 255.1(b).]

Example 2: A TV commercial depicts two women in a supermarket buying a laundry detergent. The women are not identified outside the context of the advertisement. One comments to the other how clean her brand makes her family's clothes, and the other then comments that she will try it because she has not been fully satisfied with her own brand. This obvious fictional dramatization of a real life situation would not be an endorsement.

Example 3: In an advertisement for a pain remedy, an announcer who is not familiar to consumers except as a spokesman for the advertising drug company praises the drug's ability to deliver fast and lasting pain relief. He purports to speak, not on the basis of his own opinions, but rather in the place of and on behalf of the drug company. The announcer's statements would not be considered an endorsement.

Example 4: A manufacturer of automobile tires hires a well-known professional automobile racing driver to deliver its advertising message in television commercials. In these commercials, the driver speaks of the smooth ride, strength, and long life of the tires. Even though the message is not expressly declared to be the personal opinion of the driver, it may nevertheless constitute an endorsement of the tires. Many consumers will recognize this individual as being primarily a racing driver and not merely a spokesperson or announcer for the advertiser. Accordingly, they may well believe the driver would not speak for an automotive product unless he actually believed in what he was saying and had personal knowledge sufficient to form that belief. Hence, they would think that the advertising message reflects the driver's personal views. This attribution of the underlying views to the driver brings the advertisement within the definition of an endorsement for purposes of this part.

Example 5: A television advertisement for a particular brand of golf balls shows a prominent and well-recognized professional golfer practicing numerous drives off the tee. This would be an endorsement by the golfer even though she makes no verbal statement in the advertisement.

Example 6: An infomercial for a home fitness system is hosted by a well-known entertainer. During the infomercial, the entertainer demonstrates the machine and states that it is the most effective and easy-to-use home exercise machine that she has ever tried. Even if she is reading from a script, this statement would be an endorsement, because consumers are likely to believe it reflects the entertainer's views.

Example 7: A television advertisement for a housewares store features a well-known female comedian and a well-known male baseball player engaging in light-hearted banter about products each one intends to purchase for the other. The comedian says that she will buy him a Brand X, portable, high-definition television so he can finally see the strike zone. He says that he will get her a Brand Y juicer so she can make juice with all the fruit and vegetables thrown at her during her performances. The comedian and baseball player are not likely to be deemed endorsers because consumers will likely realize that the individuals are not expressing their own views.

Example 8: A consumer who regularly purchases a particular brand of dog food decides one day to purchase a new, more expensive brand made by the same manufacturer. She writes in her personal blog that the change in diet has made her dog's fur noticeably softer and shinier, and that in her opinion, the new food definitely is worth the extra money. This posting would not be deemed an endorsement under the Guides.

Assume that rather than purchase the dog food with her own money, the consumer gets it for free because the store routinely tracks her purchases and its computer has generated a coupon for a free trial bag of this new brand. Again, her posting would not be deemed an endorsement under the Guides.

Assume now that the consumer joins a network marketing program under which she periodically receives various products about which she can write reviews if she wants to do so. If she receives a free bag of the new dog food through this program, her positive review would be considered an endorsement under the Guides.

§ 255.1   General considerations.

(a) Endorsements must reflect the honest opinions, findings, beliefs, or experience of the endorser. Furthermore, an endorsement may not convey any express or implied representation that would be deceptive if made directly by the advertiser. [*See* §§ 255.2(a) and (b) regarding substantiation of representations conveyed by consumer endorsements. (b) The endorsement message need not be phrased in the exact words of the endorser, unless the advertisement affirmatively so represents. However, the endorsement may not be presented out of context or reworded so as to distort in any way the endorser's opinion or experience with the product. An advertiser may use an endorsement of an expert or celebrity only so long as it has good reason to believe that the endorser continues to subscribe to the views presented. An advertiser may satisfy this obligation by securing the endorser's views at reasonable intervals where reasonableness will be determined by such factors as new information on the performance or effectiveness of the product, a material alteration in the product, changes in the performance of competitors' products, and the advertiser's contract commitments.

(c) When the advertisement represents that the endorser uses the endorsed product, the endorser must have been a bona fide user of it at the time the endorsement was given. Additionally, the advertiser may continue to run the advertisement only so long as it has good reason to believe that the endorser remains a bona fide user of the product. [*See* § 255.1(b) regarding the "good reason to believe" requirement.]

(d) Advertisers are subject to liability for false or unsubstantiated statements made through endorsements, or for failing to disclose material connections between themselves and their endorsers [*see* § 255.5]. Endorsers also may be liable for statements made in the course of their endorsements.

Example 1: A building contractor states in an advertisement that he uses the advertiser's exterior house paint because of its remarkable quick drying properties and durability. This endorsement must comply with the pertinent requirements of Section 255.3 (Expert Endorsements). Subsequently, the advertiser reformulates its paint to enable it to cover exterior surfaces with only one coat. Prior to continued use of the contractor's endorsement, the advertiser must contact the contractor in order to determine whether the contractor would continue to specify the paint and to subscribe to the views presented previously.

Example 2: A television advertisement portrays a woman seated at a desk on which rest five unmarked computer keyboards. An announcer says, "We asked X, an administrative assistant for over ten years, to try these five unmarked keyboards and tell us which one she liked best." The advertisement portrays X typing on each keyboard and then picking the advertiser's brand. The announcer asks her why, and X gives her reasons. This endorsement would probably not represent that X actually uses the advertiser's keyboard at work. In addition, the endorsement also may be required to meet the standards of Section 255.3 (expert endorsements).

Example 3: An ad for an acne treatment features a dermatologist who claims that the product is "clinically proven" to work. Before giving the endorsement, she received a write-up of the clinical study in question, which indicates flaws in the design and conduct of the study that are so serious that they preclude any conclusions about the efficacy of the product. The dermatologist is subject to liability for the false statements she made in the advertisement. The advertiser is also liable for misrepresentations made through the endorsement. [*See* Section 255.3 regarding the product evaluation that an expert endorser must conduct.]

Example 4: A well-known celebrity appears in an infomercial for an oven roasting bag that purportedly cooks every chicken perfectly in thirty minutes. During the shooting of the infomercial, the celebrity watches five attempts to cook chickens using the bag. In each attempt, the chicken is undercooked after thirty minutes and requires sixty minutes of cooking time. In the commercial, the celebrity places an uncooked chicken in the oven roasting bag and places the bag in one oven. He then takes a chicken roasting bag from a second oven, removes from the bag what appears to be a perfectly cooked chicken, tastes the chicken, and says that if you want perfect chicken every time, in just thirty minutes, this is the product you need. A significant percentage of consumers are likely to believe the celebrity's statements represent his own views even though he is reading from a script. The celebrity is subject to liability for his statement about the product. The advertiser is also liable for misrepresentations made through the endorsement.

Example 5: A skin care products advertiser participates in a blog advertising service. The service matches up advertisers with bloggers who will promote the advertiser's products on their personal blogs. The advertiser requests that a blogger try a new body lotion and write a review of the product on her blog. Although the advertiser does not make any specific claims about the lotion's ability to cure skin conditions and the blogger does not ask the advertiser whether there is substantiation for the claim, in her review the blogger writes that the lotion cures eczema and recommends the product to her blog readers who suffer from this condition. The advertiser is subject to liability for misleading or unsubstantiated

255.2 §

representations made through the blogger's endorsement. The blogger also is subject to liability for misleading or unsubstantiated representations made in the course of her endorsement. The blogger is also liable if she fails to disclose clearly and conspicuously that she is being paid for her services. [*See* § 255.5.]

In order to limit its potential liability, the advertiser should ensure that the advertising service provides guidance and training to its bloggers concerning the need to ensure that statements they make are truthful and substantiated. The advertiser should also monitor bloggers who are being paid to promote its products and take steps necessary to halt the continued publication of deceptive representations when they are discovered.

Consumer endorsements.

(a) An advertisement employing endorsements by one or more consumers about the performance of an advertised product or service will be interpreted as representing that the product or service is effective for the purpose depicted in the advertisement. Therefore, the advertiser must possess and rely upon adequate substantiation, including, when appropriate, competent and reliable scientific evidence, to support such claims made through endorsements in the same manner the advertiser would be required to do if it had made the representation directly, *i.e.*, without using endorsements. Consumer endorsements themselves are not competent and reliable scientific evidence.

(b) An advertisement containing an endorsement relating the experience of one or more consumers on a central or key attribute of the product or service also will likely be interpreted as representing that the endorser's experience is representative of what consumers will generally achieve with the advertised product or service in actual, albeit variable, conditions of use. Therefore, an advertiser should possess and rely upon adequate substantiation for this representation. If the advertiser does not have substantiation that the endorser's experience is representative of what consumers will generally achieve, the advertisement should clearly and conspicuously disclose the generally expected performance in the depicted circumstances, and the advertiser must possess and rely on adequate substantiation for that representation.[1]

The Commission tested the communication of advertisements containing testimonials that clearly and prominently disclosed either "Results not typical" or the stronger "These testimonials are based on the experiences of a few people and you are not likely to have similar results." Neither disclosure adequately reduced the communication that the experiences depicted are generally representative. Based upon this research, the Commission believes that similar disclaimers regarding the limited applicability of an endorser's experience to what consumers may generally expect to achieve are unlikely to be effective.

Nonetheless, the Commission cannot rule out the possibility that a strong disclaimer of typicality could be effective in the context of a particular advertisement. Although the Commission would have the burden of proof in a law enforcement action, the Commission notes that an advertiser possessing reliable empirical testing demonstrating that the net impression of its advertisement with such a disclaimer is non-deceptive will avoid the risk of the initiation of such an action in the first instance.

(c) Advertisements presenting endorsements by what are represented, directly or by implication, to be "actual consumers" should utilize actual consumers in both the audio and video, or clearly and conspicuously disclose that the persons in such advertisements are not actual consumers of the advertised product.

Example 1: A brochure for a baldness treatment consists entirely of testimonials from satisfied customers who say that after using the product, they had amazing hair growth and their hair is as thick and strong as it was when they were teenagers. The advertiser must have competent and reliable scientific evidence that its product is effective in producing new hair growth.

The ad will also likely communicate that the endorsers' experiences are representative of what new users of the product can generally expect. Therefore, even if the advertiser includes a disclaimer such as, "Notice:

These testimonials do not prove our product works. You should not expect to have similar results," the ad is likely to be deceptive unless the advertiser has adequate substantiation that new users typically will experience results similar to those experienced by the testimonialists.

Example 2: An advertisement disseminated by a company that sells heat pumps presents endorsements from three individuals who state that after installing the company's heat pump in their homes, their monthly utility bills went down by $100, $125, and $150, respectively. The ad will likely be interpreted as conveying that such savings are representative of what consumers who buy the company's heat pump can generally expect. The advertiser does not have substantiation for that representation because, in fact, less than 20% of purchasers will save $100 or more. A disclosure such as, "Results not typical" or, "These testimonials are based on the experiences of a few people and you are not likely to have similar results" is insufficient to prevent this ad from being deceptive because consumers will still interpret the ad as conveying that the specified savings are representative of what consumers can generally expect. The ad is less likely to be deceptive if it clearly and conspicuously discloses the generally expected savings and the advertiser has adequate substantiation that homeowners can achieve those results. There are multiple ways that such a disclosure could be phrased, *e.g.*, "the average homeowner saves $35 per month," "the typical family saves $50 per month during cold months and $20 per month in warm months," or "most families save 10% on their utility bills."

Example 3: An advertisement for a cholesterol-lowering product features an individual who claims that his serum cholesterol went down by 120 points and does not mention having made any lifestyle changes. A well-conducted clinical study shows that the product reduces the cholesterol levels of individuals with elevated cholesterol by an average of 15% and the advertisement clearly and conspicuously discloses this fact. Despite the presence of this disclosure, the advertisement would be deceptive if the advertiser does not have adequate substantiation that the product can produce the specific results claimed by the endorser (*i.e.*, a 120-point drop in serum cholesterol without any lifestyle changes).

Example 4: An advertisement for a weight-loss product features a formerly obese woman. She says in the ad, "Every day, I drank 2 WeightAway shakes, ate only raw vegetables, and exercised vigorously for six hours at the gym. By the end of six months, I had gone from 250 pounds to 140 pounds." The advertisement accurately describes the woman's experience, and such a result is within the range that would be generally experienced by an extremely overweight individual who consumed WeightAway shakes, only ate raw vegetables, and exercised as the endorser did. Because the endorser clearly describes the limited and truly exceptional circumstances under which she achieved her results, the ad is not likely to convey that consumers who weigh substantially less or use WeightAway under less extreme circumstances will lose 110 pounds in six months. (If the advertisement simply says that the endorser lost 110 pounds in six months using WeightAway together with diet and exercise, however, this description would not adequately alert consumers to the truly remarkable circumstances leading to her weight loss.) The advertiser must have substantiation, however, for any performance claims conveyed by the endorsement (*e.g.*, that WeightAway is an effective weight loss product).

If, in the alternative, the advertisement simply features "before" and "after" pictures of a woman who says "I lost 50 pounds in 6 months with WeightAway," the ad is likely to convey that her experience is representative of what consumers will generally achieve. Therefore, if consumers cannot generally expect to achieve such results, the ad should clearly and conspicuously disclose what they can expect to lose in the depicted circumstances (*e.g.*, "most women who use WeightAway for six months lose at least 15 pounds").

If the ad features the same pictures but the testimonialist simply says, "I lost 50 pounds with WeightAway," and WeightAway users generally do not lose 50 pounds, the ad should disclose what results they do generally achieve (*e.g.,* "most women who use WeightAway lose 15 pounds").

Example 5: An advertisement presents the results of a poll of consumers who have used the advertiser's cake mixes as well as their own recipes. The results purport to show that the majority believed that their families could not tell the difference between the advertised mix and their own cakes baked from scratch. Many of the consumers are actually pictured in the advertisement along with relevant, quoted portions of their statements endorsing the product. This use of the results of a poll or survey of consumers represents that this is the typical result that ordinary consumers can expect from the advertiser's cake mix.

Example 6: An advertisement purports to portray a "hidden camera" situation in a crowded cafeteria at breakfast time. A spokesperson for the advertiser asks a series of actual patrons of the cafeteria for their spontaneous, honest opinions of the advertiser's recently introduced breakfast cereal. Even though the words "hidden camera" are not displayed on the screen, and even though none of the actual patrons is specifically identified during the advertisement, the net impression conveyed to consumers may well be that these are actual customers, and not actors. If actors have been employed, this fact should be clearly and conspicuously disclosed.

Example 7: An advertisement for a recently released motion picture shows three individuals coming out of a theater, each of whom gives a positive statement about the movie. These individuals are actual consumers expressing their personal views about the movie. The advertiser does not need to have substantiation that their views are representative of the opinions that most consumers will have about the movie. Because the consumers' statements would be understood to be the subjective opinions of only three people, this advertisement is not likely to convey a typicality message.

If the motion picture studio had approached these individuals outside the theater and offered them free tickets if they would talk about the movie on camera afterwards, that arrangement should be clearly and conspicuously disclosed. [*See* § 255.5.]

§ 255.3   Expert endorsements.

(a) Whenever an advertisement represents, directly or by implication, that the endorser is an expert with respect to the endorsement message, then the endorser's qualifications must in fact give the endorser the expertise that he or she is represented as possessing with respect to the endorsement.

(b) Although the expert may, in endorsing a product, take into account factors not within his or her expertise (*e.g.*, matters of taste or price), the endorsement must be supported by an actual exercise of that expertise in evaluating product features or characteristics with respect to which he or she is expert and which are relevant to an ordinary consumer's use of or experience with the product and are available to the ordinary consumer. This evaluation must have included an examination or testing of the product at least as extensive as someone with the same degree of expertise would normally need to conduct in order to support the conclusions presented in the endorsement. To the extent that the advertisement implies that the endorsement was based upon a comparison, such comparison must have been included in the expert's evaluation; and as a result of such comparison, the expert must have concluded that, with respect to those features on which he or she is expert and which are relevant and available to an ordinary consumer, the endorsed product is at least equal overall to the competitors' products. Moreover, where the net impression created by the endorsement is that the advertised product is superior to other products with respect to any such feature or features, then the expert must in fact have found such superiority. [*See* § 255.1(d) regarding the liability of endorsers.]

Example 1: An endorsement of a particular automobile by one described as an "engineer" implies that the endorser's professional training and experience are such that he is well acquainted with the design and performance of automobiles. If the endorser's field is, for example, chemical engineering, the endorsement would be deceptive.

Example 2: An endorser of a hearing aid is simply referred to as "Doctor" during the course of an advertisement. The ad likely implies that the endorser is a medical doctor with substantial experience in the area of hearing. If the endorser is not a medical doctor with substantial experience in audiology, the endorsement would likely be deceptive. A non-medical "doctor" (*e.g.*, an individual with a Ph.D. in exercise physiology) or a physician without substantial experience in the area of hearing can endorse the product, but if the endorser is referred to as "doctor," the advertisement must make clear the nature and limits of the endorser's expertise.

Example 3: A manufacturer of automobile parts advertises that its products are approved by the "American Institute of Science." From its name, consumers would infer that the "American Institute of Science" is a bona fide independent testing organization with expertise in judging automobile parts and that, as such, it would not approve any automobile part without first testing its efficacy by means of valid scientific methods. If the American Institute of Science is not such a bona fide independent testing organization (*e.g.*, if it was established and operated by an automotive parts manufacturer), the endorsement would be deceptive. Even if the American Institute of Science is an independent bona fide expert testing organization, the endorsement may nevertheless be deceptive unless the Institute has conducted valid scientific tests of the advertised products and the test results support the endorsement message.

Example 4: A manufacturer of a non-prescription drug product represents that its product has been selected over competing products by a large metropolitan hospital. The hospital has selected the product because the manufacturer, unlike its competitors, has packaged each dose of the product separately. This package form is not generally available to the public. Under the circumstances, the endorsement would be deceptive because the basis for the hospital's choice – convenience of packaging – is neither relevant nor available to consumers, and the basis for the hospital's decision is not disclosed to consumers.

Example 5: A woman who is identified as the president of a commercial "home cleaning service" states in a television advertisement that the service uses a particular brand of cleanser, instead of leading competitors it has tried, because of this brand's performance. Because cleaning services extensively use cleansers in the course of their business, the ad likely conveys that the president has knowledge superior to that of ordinary consumers. Accordingly, the president's statement will be deemed to be an expert endorsement. The service must, of course, actually use the endorsed cleanser. In addition, because the advertisement implies that the cleaning service has experience with a reasonable number of leading competitors to the advertised cleanser, the service must, in fact, have such experience, and, on the basis of its expertise, it must have determined that the cleaning ability of the endorsed cleanser is at least equal (or superior, if such is the net impression conveyed by the advertisement) to that of leading competitors' products with which the service has had experience and which remain reasonably available to it. Because in this example the cleaning service's president makes no mention that the endorsed cleanser was "chosen," "selected," or otherwise evaluated in side-by-side comparisons against its competitors, it is sufficient if the service has relied solely upon its accumulated experience in evaluating cleansers without having performed side-by-side or scientific comparisons.

Example 6: A medical doctor states in an advertisement for a drug that the product will safely allow consumers to lower their cholesterol by 50 points. If the materials the doctor reviewed were merely letters from satisfied consumers or the results of a rodent study, the endorsement would likely be deceptive because those materials are not what others with the same degree of expertise would consider adequate to support this conclusion about the product's safety and efficacy.

§ 255.4   Endorsements by organizations.

Endorsements by organizations, especially expert ones, are viewed as representing the judgment of a group whose collective experience exceeds that of any individual member, and whose judgments are generally free of the sort of subjective factors that vary from individual to individual. Therefore, an organization's endorsement must be reached by a process sufficient to ensure that the endorsement fairly reflects the collective judgment of the organization. Moreover, if an organization is represented as being expert, then, in conjunction with a proper exercise of its expertise in evaluating the product under § 255.3 (expert endorsements), it must utilize an expert or experts recognized as such by the organization or standards previously adopted by the organization and suitable for judging the relevant merits of such products. [*See* § 255.1(d) regarding the liability of endorsers.]

Example: A mattress seller advertises that its product is endorsed by a chiropractic association. Because the association would be regarded as expert with respect to judging mattresses, its endorsement must be supported by an evaluation by an expert or experts recognized as such by the organization, or by compliance with standards previously adopted by the organization and aimed at measuring the performance of mattresses in general and not designed with the unique features of the advertised mattress in mind.

§ 255.5   Disclosure of material connections.

When there exists a connection between the endorser and the seller of the advertised product that might materially affect the weight or credibility of the endorsement (*i.e.*, the connection is not reasonably expected by the audience), such connection must be fully disclosed. For example, when an endorser who appears in a television commercial is neither represented in the advertisement as an expert nor is known to a significant portion of the viewing public, then the advertiser should clearly and conspicuously disclose either the payment or promise of compensation prior to and in exchange for the endorsement or the fact that the endorser knew or had reason to know or to believe that if the endorsement favored the advertised product some benefit, such as an appearance on television, would be extended to the endorser. Additional guidance, including guidance concerning endorsements made through other media, is provided by the examples below.

Example 1: A drug company commissions research on its product by an outside organization. The drug company determines the overall subject of the research (*e.g.*, to test the efficacy of a newly developed product) and pays a substantial share of the expenses of the research project, but the research organization determines the protocol for the study and is responsible for conducting it. A subsequent advertisement by the drug company mentions the research results as the "findings" of that research organization. Although the design and conduct of the research project are controlled by the outside research organization, the weight consumers place on the reported results could be materially affected by knowing that the advertiser had funded the project. Therefore, the advertiser's payment of expenses to the research organization should be disclosed in this advertisement.

Example 2: A film star endorses a particular food product. The endorsement regards only points of taste and individual preference. This endorsement must, of course, comply with § 255.1; but regardless of whether the star's compensation for the commercial is a $1 million cash payment or a royalty for each product sold by the advertiser during the next year, no disclosure is required because such payments likely are ordinarily expected by viewers.

Example 3: During an appearance by a well-known professional tennis player on a television talk show, the host comments that the past few months have been the best of her career and during this time she has risen to her highest level ever in the rankings. She responds by attributing the improvement in her game to the fact that she is seeing the ball better than she used to, ever since having laser vision correction surgery at a clinic that she identifies by name. She continues talking about the ease of the procedure, the kindness of the clinic's doctors, her speedy recovery, and how she can now engage in a variety of activities without glasses, including driving at night. The athlete does not disclose that, even though she does not appear in commercials for the clinic, she has a contractual relationship with it, and her contract pays her for speaking publicly about her surgery when she can do so. Consumers might not realize that a celebrity discussing a medical procedure in a television interview has been paid for doing so, and knowledge of such payments would likely affect the weight or credibility consumers give to the celebrity's endorsement. Without a clear and conspicuous disclosure that the athlete has been engaged as a spokesperson for the clinic, this endorsement is likely to be deceptive. Furthermore, if consumers are likely to take away from her story that her experience was typical of those who undergo the same procedure at the clinic, the advertiser must have substantiation for that claim.

Assume that instead of speaking about the clinic in a television interview, the tennis player touts the results of her surgery – mentioning the clinic by name – on a social networking site that allows her fans to read in real time what is happening in her life. Given the nature of the medium in which her endorsement is disseminated, consumers might not realize that she is a paid endorser. Because that information might affect the weight consumers give to her endorsement, her relationship with the clinic should be disclosed.

Assume that during that same television interview, the tennis player is wearing clothes bearing the insignia of an athletic wear company with whom she also has an endorsement contract. Although this contract requires that she wear the company's clothes not only on the court but also in public appearances, when possible, she does not mention them or the company during her appearance on the show. No disclosure is required because no representation is being made about the clothes in this context.

Example 4: An ad for an anti-snoring product features a physician who says that he has seen dozens of products come on the market over the years and, in his opinion, this is the best ever. Consumers would expect the physician to be reasonably compensated for his appearance in the ad. Consumers are unlikely, however, to expect that the physician receives a percentage of gross product sales or that he owns part of the company, and either of these facts would likely materially affect the credibility that consumers attach to the endorsement. Accordingly, the advertisement should clearly and conspicuously disclose such a connection between the company and the physician.

Example 5: An actual patron of a restaurant, who is neither known to the public nor presented as an expert, is shown seated at the counter. He is asked for his "spontaneous" opinion of a new food product served in the restaurant. Assume, first, that the advertiser had posted a sign on the door of the restaurant informing all who entered that day that patrons would be interviewed by the advertiser as part of its TV promotion of its new soy protein "steak." This notification would materially affect the weight or credibility of the patron's endorsement, and, therefore, viewers of the advertisement should be clearly and conspicuously informed of the circumstances under which the endorsement was obtained.

Assume, in the alternative, that the advertiser had not posted a sign on the door of the restaurant, but had informed all interviewed customers of the "hidden camera" only after interviews were completed and the customers had no reason to know or believe that their response was being recorded for use in an advertisement. Even if patrons were also told that they would be paid for allowing the use of their opinions in advertising, these facts need not be disclosed.

Example 6: An infomercial producer wants to include consumer endorsements for an automotive additive product featured in her commercial, but because the product has not yet been sold, there are no consumer users. The producer's staff reviews the profiles of individuals interested in working as "extras" in commercials and identifies several who are interested in automobiles. The extras are asked to use the product for several weeks and then report back to the producer. They are told that if they are selected to endorse the product in the producer's infomercial, they will receive a small payment. Viewers would not expect that these "consumer endorsers" are actors who were asked to use the product so that they could appear in the commercial or that they were compensated. Because the advertisement fails to disclose these facts, it is deceptive.

Example 7: A college student who has earned a reputation as a video game expert maintains a personal weblog or "blog" where he posts entries about his gaming experiences. Readers of his blog frequently seek his opinions about video game hardware and software. As it has done in the past, the manufacturer of a newly released video game system sends the student a free copy of the system and asks him to write about it on his blog. He tests the new gaming system and writes a favorable review. Because his review is disseminated via a form of consumer-generated media in which his relationship to the advertiser is not inherently obvious, readers are unlikely to know that he has received the video game system free of charge in exchange for his review of the product, and given the value of the video game system, this fact likely would materially affect the credibility they attach to his endorsement. Accordingly, the blogger should clearly and conspicuously disclose that he received the gaming system free of charge. The manufacturer should advise him at the time it provides the gaming system that this connection should be disclosed, and it should have procedures in place to try to monitor his postings for compliance.

Example 8: An online message board designated for discussions of new music download technology is frequented by MP3 player enthusiasts. They exchange information about new products, utilities, and the functionality of numerous playback devices. Unbeknownst to the message board community, an employee of a leading playback device manufacturer has been posting messages on the discussion board promoting the manufacturer's product. Knowledge of this poster's employment likely would affect the weight or credibility of her endorsement. Therefore, the poster should clearly and conspicuously disclose her relationship to the manufacturer to members and readers of the message board.

Example 9: A young man signs up to be part of a "street team" program in which points are awarded each time a team member talks to his or her friends about a particular advertiser's products. Team members can then exchange their points for prizes, such as concert tickets or electronics. These incentives would materially affect the weight or credibility of the team member's endorsements. They should be clearly and conspicuously disclosed, and the advertiser should take steps to ensure that these disclosures are being provided.

Breinigsville, PA USA
01 December 2010
250425BV00005B/18/P

For Baby J
who we waited for
for so long